prophetic vessel in the earth
that are included are keys fo
prophetic gift that lies withi

Dr. Chuck D. Pierce, president, Glory of Zion International, Kingdom Harvest Alliance, and Global Spheres

"Cindy Jacobs teaches the proper way of exercising the gift she has used publicly during a renowned ministry career that has spanned decades. Prophecy was never intended to be limited to those in the pulpit. It is also for those in the pew. I encourage you to study this book, learn how to exercise your gift, and become an integral part of God's solution to healing our world."

Samuel Rodriguez , lead pastor, New Season Worship; president/CEO, National Hispanic Christian Leadership Conference; author, *Persevere with Power*; executive producer, *Breakthrough* and *Flamin' Hot*

"Never has there been a more crucial time to clearly hear the voice of God. Confusion, chaos, and a cacophony of other voices muddy the modern waters of needed direction. Yet heaven has ordained a fresh clarity and a new discernment to weaponize our witness and solidify our faith. Cindy Jacobs has provided a strategic masterpiece and has modeled a keen and healthy biblical ministry of the prophetic. I highly recommend this astounding book."

Sean Smith, co-director, Sean & Christa Smith Ministries; author, *Prophetic Evangelism* and *I Am Your Sign*

"Cindy Jacobs clearly articulates the complex topic of prophecy in a way that is approachable, revelatory, and inspiring no matter where you are on your prophetic journey. I would highly recommend this book to anyone hungry to discover the voice of God and grow in their prophetic gifting!"

Kris Vallotton, co-founder, Bethel School of Supernatural Ministry; author, *The Supernatural Ways of Royalty*, *Spirit Wars*, *Uprising* and more; senior associate leader, Bethel Church, Redding, California of the prophetic. Her prophetic gift has provided direction and clarity in the most profound ways. *The Essential Guide to the Prophetic* is the book we all need. Cindy has the unique anointing to equip and also activate people in this gift with practical and insightful techniques. I have no doubt this book will position you to hear God's voice clearly."

Banning Liebscher, founder and pastor, Jesus Culture

"As a pioneer in the prophetic, there is no better leader to learn from than Cindy Jacobs. Her invaluable mentorship on the topic makes *The Essential Guide to the Prophetic* a wellspring of revelation and your new go-to resource for prophecy. Prepare to be equipped and trained like never before!"

Apostle Guillermo Maldonado, main pastor,
King Jesus Ministry, Miami, Florida

"*The Essential Guide to the Prophetic* is filled with wisdom for the end-time prophetic generation. Young prophets and those mature in their gift will glean from Cindy's teaching and be impacted by her personal journey as a prophet. This handbook is a must-read!"

Jonathan and Sharon Ngai, founders and directors,
Radiance International and Hollywood House of Prayer

"I know of no one better qualified to write *The Essential Guide to the Prophetic* than Cindy Jacobs. She was the most significant prophetic mentor of my life. In this book you have a guide that will enable you to become an incredible

"The general has done it again! Cindy Jacobs was born to be a pioneer, a forerunner, and to lead the way so that other believers could cross over into the fullness of their destiny. . . . Two things I love most about *The Essential Guide to the Prophetic* are the application section at the end of each chapter and how Cindy always insists on developing character to carry the gift. The only thing I can add to this essential prophetic manual is a loud AMEN! Well done, good and faithful steward. The next generation will be richly blessed!"

James W. Goll, founder, God Encounters
Ministries and GOLL Ideations

"This is an absolutely wonderful book! Seriously. It just might become the handbook of a generation that is called to bring the word of the Lord into the darkest places of earth. The word of the Lord is what sets people free. When I think of a seasoned prophet, I think of Cindy Jacobs. And through all the fires of difficulty she has experienced in her lifetime, she stands strong, with an absolute confidence in the goodness of God. From that place of assurance, she gives us a profoundly practical guide to the prophetic, which is perfectly fit for every believer. Please prayerfully devour this book."

Bill Johnson, senior leader, Bethel Church, Redding, CA;
author, *Open Heavens* and *Born for Significance*

"The voice of God is our inheritance. Sadly, for many, the prophetic has become a minefield of neglect, confusion, abuse, and bad doctrine. I cannot think of anyone better than Cindy Jacobs to mentor a generation in the essentials

THE
ESSENTIAL
GUIDE
TO THE
PROPHETIC

HOW TO HEAR
THE VOICE OF GOD

CINDY
JACOBS

Chosen
a division of Baker Publishing Group
Minneapolis, Minnesota

© 1995, 2016, 2022 by Cindy Jacobs

Published by Chosen Books
11400 Hampshire Avenue South
Minneapolis, Minnesota 55438
www.chosenbooks.com

Chosen Books is a division of
Baker Publishing Group, Grand Rapids, Michigan

Printed in the United States of America

Library of Congress Cataloging-in-Publication Data

Names: Jacobs, Cindy, author.
Title: The essential guide to the prophetic : how to hear the voice of God / Cindy Jacobs.
Other titles: Voice of God
Description: Minneapolis, Minnesota : Chosen Books, a division of Baker Publishing Group, 2022. | Includes bibliographical references.
Identifiers: LCCN 2022023757 | ISBN 9780800762728 (trade paper) | ISBN 9780800762896 (casebound) | ISBN 9781493438686 (ebook)
Subjects: LCSH: Prophecy—Christianity.
Classification: LCC BR115.P8 J33 2022 | DDC 234/.13—dc23/eng/20220705
LC record available at https://lccn.loc.gov/2022023757

Content adapted from *The Voice of God*

Cover design by Rob Williams, InsideOut Creative Arts, Inc.

Baker Publishing Group publications use paper produced from sustainable forestry practices and post-consumer waste whenever possible.

22 23 24 25 26 27 28   7 6 5 4 3 2 1

CONTENTS

INTRODUCTION

For many years, there has been a common theme in my life. It usually starts with someone writing me and saying, "Cindy, I need a mentor in my life! I want to know about how to hear God's voice." Or, similarly, "Cindy, I know I have the gift of prophecy, but I don't know how to use it. Will you mentor me?"

This has been sad to me. Of course, I would like to respond with a yes, but that is simply not physically possible. This essential guide comes with my yearning to be able to help you along your journey to both hear God's voice and to know what to do and how to answer when you do so.

As I look back over what could be called sixty-plus years of prophesying (I first prophesied when I was four years old), I can see that I have made my share of mistakes. Thankfully, with the making of those mistakes comes learning from them. The good thing is that you don't have to run into a wall at full speed as many times as I have.

This book could be called *Gleanings*. I have taken the best nuggets of what I have learned about the prophetic and intercession (for they are interwoven) and given them to you.

When I first started to prophesy in earnest, when I sort of began to understand what I was doing, I searched for material on the prophetic. This was in the late '70s and early '80s. At first, I only found the classic book by John and Paula Sandford called *The Elijah Task*. I must admit that the first time I read it, it was Greek to me. The concepts they wrote about were just beyond my understanding! I simply did not have enough grasp of the prophetic to have even an inkling as to what they were writing about. Thankfully, a few years later, I had grown considerably in my biblical maturity and read it with understanding.

In the '80s, my now good friend Bishop Bill Hamon wrote his brilliant prophetic series, *Prophets and Personal Prophecy*. By that time, I was prophesying quite a bit myself and had a traveling ministry. I then went on to write my book *The Voice of God* in 1995.

The book that you are holding in your hands contains material from all of my journey. It is practical and easy to understand. You will find answers to many of your questions. I wanted it to feel as if I am sitting down with you in a one-to-one conversation, and you were saying, "Well, Cindy, what about _____, or what about _____?"

Some of my personal stories are included. A good mentoring book always invites you to share the life of the person you are receiving mentoring from.

Many times people ask me, "Cindy, how have you risen through your years of ministry to be known around the world as an intercessor and prophet?" Of course, number one would be my personal relationship with the Lord. But another big reason is that I have studied. Being a student involves time and personal discipline. It is not for the lazy!

I have a personal spiritual ambition for you as you read this book. I want it to change your life! I desire that you will be a different person when you finish reading it and that you will apply what you have learned. Not only for you, the individual, but also for you, the Christian, who wants to make a difference in people's lives by hearing the voice of God.

Let's go on an adventure!

Love and blessings,
Cindy

— 1 —

The Voice of God

Do you believe that God speaks to you?

It's a fundamental question that so many people ask themselves at least once. The truth is, God communicates with His sons and daughters. Think of how He spoke in both the Old and New Testaments to and through ordinary people like Moses, Gideon, Samuel, Philip, and the apostle John. At times, He even spoke to those who had rejected Him and who were not yet His own, as He did with Saul on the road to Damascus, or the Pharaoh of Egypt who dreamed of the seven years of plenty and seven years of famine. Did you know, though, that through His Holy Spirit, His Word, and His people, God speaks today, just as He did thousands of years ago?

As Christians, we believe that the Holy Bible is the infallible Word of God. It is His perfect communication to us and contains His one and only path for salvation. However, God also speaks to believers on a personal level, as He always has. We don't have to long for the Old Testament days when God spoke with His prophets directly; He is speaking right now.

If you are not used to listening for His voice, or if you are new in your walk with Christ, the idea of hearing from God or receiving a prophetic word may be overwhelming. Maybe the word "prophecy" feels uncomfortable because the topic was never discussed in your church, or perhaps you have had negative experiences encountering people operating in prophetic ministry. Prophecy can feel daunting, mysterious, and at times overwhelming, but please be encouraged! In 1 Corinthians 14:33, we see "For God is not a God of confusion but of peace" (NASB1995). He desires to be heard and understood by His children. God wants to speak to you, and the process of learning to hear His voice can be sweet, powerful, and deeply intimate.

This handbook is designed to be a guide along your journey. We will highlight the different ways God speaks, what it means to give or receive a prophecy, how we discern if a word is from God, and how to cultivate the prophetic gift. Our ultimate goal is to hear His voice and use His gifts in a way that brings Him glory, and brings encouragement and growth to God's Church. Let's begin!

So what *does* it mean to hear the voice of God?

When I was just four years old, I crawled onto my mother's lap and declared, "Mama, I want a baby sister." My mother laughed and said "Sweetheart, we're not having any more children. You're the last one!" My parents were not planning on having more children, but I insisted that Mama was going to have a baby girl. The next year, my sister Lucy was born.

Of course, I had no idea at age four what my "knowing" was; I just stated what I sensed. I remember other times when the phone would ring in our house, and someone had a serious message, and I would know before the phone rang what had happened. Now I understand that, at a young age, the Lord was using me in the area of prophecy and prophetic intercession. However, at the time, I did not understand what to do with what I was receiving or why it was happening.

I was hearing the voice of God.

In addition to God's Word (the Bible), these are the ways we see God speaking to His children:

- Through a knowing, or a strong impression. You may suddenly know details about something you had no previous knowledge of, or you may know about something that hasn't happened yet but is later confirmed.

- In a spontaneous phrase or message that comes to mind. Sometimes this will be a Scripture, a simple sentence, or a longer message.

- In an audible voice like Paul (then Saul) experienced on the road to Damascus, or Moses heard coming from the burning bush.

- Through dreams and visions. We will dive deeper into this topic in later chapters, but God still speaks today through dreams and visions like He did to Joseph in the Old Testament.
- By a prophetic word delivered to you by another believer. Just as in the days of God's prophets, you can receive a prophetic word from another believer.

Discerning God's Voice from Other Voices

Our world is very noisy, and all that confusion and clamoring can sometimes leave us wondering, "Was that me I just heard, or was that God?" Something I would encourage you to do as you begin to tune your ears to God's voice is to find a quiet place to talk with God. That may feel like a challenge in and of itself, but finding a place and time to be still and listen is very important.

When I was nine years old, I attended a junior church camp in Arizona. At my camp counselor's suggestion, I went off on my own to find a quiet place to talk to God. I crawled up on a huge rock outside of our chapel, and as I lay on that rough granite rock, looking up at the artistry of God painted across the blue sky and towering trees, I prayed, "Lord, what do You want from my life?" At first, all I heard was the sound of the wind and trees harmonizing with the birds in the woods. Then I heard another quiet sound—it was the voice of God saying, "*Cindy, I have something I want you to do for Me.*" At the sound of His voice speaking so sweetly in my soul, I responded with my heart beating a staccato along with the wind and trees, "Here am I, Lord; send me." I was just a child, but I was learning to be still and listen for His voice, to take time to press in, and to identify when He was the one speaking.

In addition to taking time to be still and listen for the voice of God, it is important to remember that these messages we receive can have three possible sources:

1. The Spirit of God
2. The spirit of error or demonic spirits
3. Our own flesh

Sometimes, in the midst of hearing the Spirit of God, our flesh will interject and add to the message. This often happens because we have a message we hope to hear, so our flesh pops it into what we are actually hearing. Later on, we will discuss in depth how to weigh and test what you are hearing, but above all else, how to ask if what you are hearing lines up with the Scriptures. God does not contradict Himself. A demonic spirit or spirit of error may also incorporate kernels of truth in the message, but ultimately, their word will not align with Scripture. It may cause feelings of anxiety, worry, condemnation, shame, and other emotions that are not of God. God's voice will always line up with His written Word and be an accurate representation of His character.

What Is Prophecy?

Prophecy can be defined as a spontaneous, divinely-given understanding or foreknowledge about a person or an event. Prophecy is one of the gifts of the Spirit that believers are to desire once they are saved and filled by the Holy Spirit. In 1 Corinthians 14:1 and 14:39, Paul encourages the Church to desire the gifts of the Spirit, but above all, the gift of prophecy.

Now, a prophecy can be simple, which means it will not be as detailed or include any foretelling. These simple prophecies are meant to be edifying, exhortative, or comforting, but they will not tell of things to come. For example, you might receive a prophecy that says something like, "The Lord sees your obedience to Him in the area of your work, and He is so pleased with how your witness stands before your colleagues. You are beloved by your heavenly Father, and He delights over you." Do you see how that is an expression of God's heart toward the person receiving the prayer?

A more complex prophecy will tell of things that are coming and could include warnings or detailed instructions for the person or church. Budding prophetic people may occasionally flow with detailed words that include foretelling, but that does not make them prophets. God's training for His prophets takes years. One leader said he believes it takes about twenty years of intensive instruction in God's boot camp before He sets a person into the office of the prophet. Now, God can of course use more or less time, but He generally puts the prophet through many years of training before releasing him or her fully. We will talk more about training in later chapters.

When we prophesy, we take what we believe we hear God saying and articulate it to others.

Think of the prophets of the Old Testament, like Samuel or Nathan. When they heard the voice of God, what did they do? They delivered it. Prophesying is the delivery of the word from God.

What is the purpose of prophesying? If we look at 1 Corinthians 14:3, we can see there are three main functions. We will discuss these further in Chapter 2.

1. Edification
2. Encouragement
3. Comfort

What does the Bible say about prophecy?

This is what I will do in the last days—I will pour out my Spirit on everybody and cause your sons and daughters to prophesy, and your young men will see visions, and your old men will experience dreams from God. The Holy Spirit will come upon all my servants, men and women alike, and they will prophesy.

Acts 2:17–18 TPT

Prophecy is intended to be an integral part of our walk with Christ. It is meant to be normal for believers and is a spiritual gift to be desired and utilized for the glory of God and the building up of His Church.

In the Bible, we see that a person can receive a prophetic word from God in a number of ways:

1. God speaking through one person to another (Acts 21:10–11)
2. The Holy Spirit speaking to an individual directly (Acts 10:19)
3. A dream or vision (Matthew 1:20; Acts 9:10–11)
4. Reading the Bible (Daniel 9:2–21)
5. Hearing a spontaneous prophetic song given from God to an individual during worship (1 Samuel 10:5; 1 Corinthians 14:15; Ephesians 5:19).

Who can prophesy?

Every person who has received the gift of salvation through the death and resurrection of Jesus Christ, and has been filled with the Holy Spirit, has the potential to operate in their prophetic gifting. For many people, this gift will not be very active until the Holy Spirit activates it and they learn to press in and listen to what God is saying. Very young children have been known to prophesy, as well as brand-new believers, once filled with the Holy Spirit.

For some believers, the prophetic will be an integral part of their ministry. For others, they may not use it often. We find different types of prophetic voices and callings throughout the Scriptures. However, believers of all ages should understand the various ways that God speaks to His people. Even if prophecy is not a gift you regularly use in ministry, you should have a biblical understanding of prophecy and the prophetic gift.

Old Testament vs. New Testament prophets

In the Old Testament, the Holy Spirit had not yet been poured out on God's people, so God spoke through His prophets. Prophets in the Old Testament were appointed, anointed spokespersons for God. When they delivered a word, they often began by saying, "This is what God is saying," because they were basically delivering a message or edict from God to His people. They held great responsibility and authority, and it was so important that they be accurate when sharing the word.

In the New Testament (and today), we are living under the outpouring of God's Holy Spirit that came at Pentecost. Today, prophecy could be sharing something that God has spontaneously brought to mind.[1] It isn't necessary to begin by saying, "This is what God is saying," because God can now speak to all of His children through the indwelling of the Holy Spirit. New Testament prophecy does not carry the authority of Scripture, but it can carry a revelation for the hour about what God wants His Church to know.

The three types of prophecy

1. Personal (or private) prophecy: This is a prophetic word from God, delivered to an individual.
2. Corporate prophecy: This is a prophetic word delivered to a body or congregation of believers.
3. Prophetic intercession: This is the ability to pray and intercede with prophetic insight and empowering from God's Spirit for specific issues God brings to mind at specific times.

Testing prophetic words: six questions to ask

Now that we understand what it means to hear God's voice, and the many ways He speaks to us, what do we do with the words we receive?

In 1 Thessalonians 5:21, we read, "Test all things; hold fast what is good." Especially in the area of prophecy, it is important that we test what we are hearing against the Scriptures. Let's remember that God never minds confirming His word to us. Remember how many questions Mary asked the angel when he announced she would be the mother of the Messiah? How many times did Gideon ask for confirmation, or how many objections did Moses give to God's Spirit speaking through the burning bush? God will not be angry if you have questions and ask Him for further confirmation.

Here are six questions you can ask when you are testing a prophetic word:

1. Is what has been shared as a prophetic word biblical? It can be easy for deception to sneak in, especially if we are personally in a vulnerable place. Ask yourself if the prophetic word you are receiving lines up with the infallible Word of God. If it's telling you to sin, or if it is in direct contrast to God's laws, you have a sure sign this is not from God.

2. Does the prophecy display the character of Christ? Are the attributes of Jesus' character, such as love, kindness, obedience, mercy, truth, and patience (just to name a few), reflected in the prophetic word being given? If the word is filled with rage, shame, or hatred, it is not lining up with the character of God.

3. What is the fruit in the life of the person giving the prophecy? Does the person operate in integrity so that what they say matches up with their life? Is their personal life in line with their public ministry life, or is it in a shambles of their own making? If you do not know the person delivering the word, ask the Holy Spirit to highlight any concerning areas. Please note: You are not being judgmental when you ask the Holy Spirit this question. Not every person operating in the prophetic gifting is in a healthy place, nor should every person be speaking into your life like this. Let the Holy Spirit give you wisdom and discernment.

4. Is anything tainting the word? If people are not whole in certain parts of their lives, or if they are unaware of their biases toward others, it can taint the prophetic word. To check for this, ask:

   • Is the person critical or judgmental? Prophetic words that are frightening, harsh, condemning, or critical are rarely from the Holy Spirit. Even if the word is one of correction, God convicts and calls His children to return to Him; He does not shame or belittle.

   • Is there any evidence of a religious bias? Some people may use prophecy to promote their "pet" doctrines. Legalism can easily slip in, especially if the person on the receiving end of the word suffers from a religious spirit.

5. What is the Holy Spirit giving you in the way of an inward witness? In John 10:27, we read that the sheep know the voice of their Shepherd. When we receive a prophetic word from the Lord, our spirits might answer back, "I know that voice!" Many times, a prophetic word can confirm something you already knew in your spirit. On the contrary, if the word you are receiving is not from God, you may feel a discomfort in your spirit that says, *That doesn't sound right* or *Something about that feels off.*

6. Is the prophecy from God? God's prophetic word will never contradict His infallible written Word in principle, character, or exact Scripture. Sometimes, the prophetic word can be a mixture of our flesh sneaking through at the same time God's Spirit is speaking. This is why it is important to test the words against Scripture.

Now What? Responding to the Prophetic Word

Often, we receive a word and jump to our own interpretation, but that can lead to mistakes and misapplications. Many people have received a word and taken it as a "NOW" word when it is actually a "wait" word.

When I was in my twenties, the Lord spoke to me through Psalm 2:8 and through His voice to my spirit that I was to "Ask of Me . . . the nations for Your inheritance, and the ends of the earth for Your possession." I responded and prayed that prayer, but it would be many years before I understood that the stirring in my heart that day was a small indicator of the ministry the Lord would someday give me. That word, and the gift of prophetic intercession on my life, came to fruition years later in God's perfect timing. The word was absolutely accurate, but the timing and interpretation would be fulfilled later.

Once you are fairly certain that the word you received is from the Lord, it needs to be interpreted accurately. This means you need to discern what God is trying to say through the prophecy.

Here are some practical steps to begin interpreting:

1. Try to record the prophetic word as the person gives it (or write it down). You may miss something key in the moment and will want to go back to listen to it. Thanks to modern technology, almost every smartphone has a built-in recording feature, so you can use that and listen to the word on your phone later.

2. Share the recorded (or written) prophecy with someone you respect and trust. Share it with an "elder" in the Spirit (someone more spiritually mature than you) who knows about testing prophecy.

3. Be careful not to interpret the word in the light of your own wants and desires. Especially if you are in a vulnerable or painful place in your life, it is easy to twist a prophetic word so it fits into your situation. Please do not do that; you will miss the fullness of what God is saying to you, and it could send you in the wrong direction.

4. What is the timing of the prophetic word? This can be one of the trickiest parts of interpreting a prophetic word? God's timing is not our timing, and as we move in faith and obedience toward His will, we also don't want to run ahead of God.

Here are a few questions to help you follow God's timing:

- Is this word consistent with everything God has been saying about my life?
- How will this affect my current responsibilities? For example, will I be able to take care of my family financially? What kind of stress will this put on my family? Are they willing to make sacrifices if I make these changes in my life?
- Have I reached a maturity level in my life that will enable me to perform with integrity the new tasks and/or changes, or will I flake out because I am not properly prepared?
- Do brothers and sisters in the Lord bear witness to this word, especially those in authority over me?

5. Believe God will fulfill the prophecy in His own time and way. You cannot strongarm a prophecy into fulfillment. You can take practical steps forward as God directs, but it is imperative that He leads. When we push too fast or try to make things happen, we risk missing key moments and opportunities He provides. Do the last thing He told you to do, and do it with excellence and faithfulness. He will reveal the next step when it is time.

APPLICATION

Grab a journal and pen or take notes on your smartphone and answer the reflection questions below.

1. Ask yourself honestly—do you think it is possible to hear the voice of God today?
2. Have you surrendered your life to be used by God in any way He sees fit for you? When did you do that? If it has been a while, take some time to see if there is any part of your life that maybe isn't surrendered. If there is, go to the Lord in prayer and surrender your whole self to Him.
3. Have you ever heard God's voice through a knowing, a phrase, a song, a dream, or a word delivered to you by a fellow believer, and did what you heard later prove to be true? Write a few sentences about that experience.

Now that you have a sense for how you have experienced God's voice in the past, take time to be alone with Him. Get comfortable in a quiet place, no distractions, and just be still. If putting in earbuds or playing some soft, instrumental music helps to focus you, do that. Be present. This can be hard, as many of us have to-do lists forming in our heads, or our thoughts are running in a hundred directions. Just focus on God's presence filling the room. If it helps to imagine Him sitting next to you, do that, and focus on His presence. Just listen. See what He has to say.

It's okay if this takes some practice, and please be gentle with yourself if quieting your mind is hard at first. Keep showing up for these moments with the Lord, and you will begin to hear His voice speak to your spirit.

— 2 —

What Is the Goal
of Prophecy?

Throughout the Scriptures, we see examples of God using different means to redeem His people unto Himself. We see in the Old Testament where God redeems His people from slavery, sin, and oppression, often using the voice of His prophets to herald that redemption. For example, in the book of Isaiah, God speaks through the prophet time after time in an effort to redeem the people of Israel from their sin and bondage.

The prophesied Messiah was redemptive. The purpose of Jesus' death and resurrection was redemptive, so the lost could be restored. God is redemptive. It shouldn't surprise us that redemption is a theme running through His messages to us.

There are times in the Bible when God speaks correction over an individual or a church body. Think of the words spoken to John in Revelation. The messages for the churches were varied, were personalized, and spoke of correction and redemption. While a corrective word can be difficult for us to hear, these words carry so much of the Father's love and desire that we be reconciled and whole in His sight. In this chapter, we will discuss the purpose of a rebuke and how this kind of word should be delivered.

When a Prophetic Word Is Redemptive

1. Redemptive prophecy speaks to the destiny of God for an individual or church body in a life-bringing, freeing, and redemptive way. When we receive a redemptive prophecy, we feel more known by God. God often will incorporate details about us that are very personal, sometimes coming from the secret places of our hearts, and emphasizing how much interest and care He takes with us. Redemptive prophecy is incredibly powerful and often brings about an increase in an individual's personal faith.

2. Redemptive conviction speaks to the good things in a person's life, their virtues, and the ways they have honored God, but it also carries a strong judgment that leads to the conviction of sin. A biblical example of this would be the prophet Nathan delivering a

word to King David after David ordered the death of Uriah to cover up his sin with Bathsheba. Nathan's prophecy before David led to conviction and repentance. Repentance and redemption are the goal.

3. Redemptive proclamation is a declaration of something God is doing or has done in a person's life, meant to encourage and shore them up in the face of doubt. It is confirming and will sometimes resonate with something the person has already sensed from the Lord. In the Bible, Gabriel's proclamation to Mary that she would be the mother of Jesus would be considered a redemptive proclamation. When she later came under scrutiny for being with child outside of marriage, the proclamation gave Mary strength. She had God's backing, and she knew it.

When God Speaks Rebuke

Have you ever avoided receiving prayer or a prophetic word because you are afraid of your secrets and sins being called out in a public place? If so, you aren't alone. When the God of the universe, who knows you intimately, wants to speak through a prophetic voice, it can be nerve-wracking. What if you are called out and publicly shamed? What if your secrets and wounds suddenly are spoken out loud for others to hear? This can feel so risky, but remember that God's desire is redemption.

31

There are rare occasions when the Lord rebukes a person or a church body through a prophetic word in a public arena. However, those public rebukes are usually preceeded by many private warnings and opportunities for repentance. The goal is never to shame, but rather to convict and redeem. The Lord will speak correction and conviction, giving the person or church many chances to repent. If that person is in extreme rebellion, they may possibly be reached through a strong prophecy, as David was by the prophet Nathan. Another good example is Moses' visits to Pharaoh. How many times did God give Pharaoh the opportunity to respond to correction? It was Pharaoh's hardness of heart that led to his downfall.

It is important for prophetic ministers to note that Nathan went to David privately to deliver the word of rebuke. He did not take to the streets and publicly drag David's name and sins. Shaming a person does not often lead to redemption. In fact, it can drive the person further from the Lord. Rebuke is not intended to be a punishment or a public shaming. The goal is redemption for the individual, and that they return to godliness and fellowship with the Lord. If the person delivering the corrective word has any animosity, bitterness, or anger in their heart toward the person receiving, or if they relish being the one to give the word because they have been wounded by the receiver, they are not the one to give that word.

Sometimes, one of the kindest things you can do for a person is to share a corrective word. However, it is important that the word be shared in a way that the person can receive it. Be sure you share the word with the love of Christ and not with the intention to slam or condemn. One of the greatest compliments I have ever received was from my friend who said, "You know, I can take it when you share corrective things with me because I know you love me." As hard as it is to hear a corrective word, knowing that it is coming from a God who loves you, and through a person who has love for you, makes it easier to take.

The Three Functions of Prophecy

What is the purpose of prophecy? If a believer can hear the voice of God, why do we also need prophetic voices?

> On the other hand, the one who prophesies speaks to people for their upbuilding and encouragement and consolation.
>
> 1 Corinthians 14:3 ESV

In this verse, Paul lays out the primary purposes of prophecy. While there can be other positive results of a prophetic word (giving glory to God, repentance, etc.), these are the three main functions.

1. Edification: This type of word is for upbuilding. Other biblical translations use the word "strengthening" in the same way you would speak about building and strengthening a house. An edifying word

33

will bring about directional change, preparation for a move of God, or conviction, but it will always be focused on building the hearer up in their faith. If a word releases discouragement, heaviness, or shame over the hearer, it is not a prophetic word from the Spirit of God. Satan never edifies, but he does try to nullify the work of God.

2. Encouragement: This type of prophecy reminds the receiver that God is in control, we have been heard by our Father in Heaven, all the promises of the Bible are for us to believe, and we are not alone. It can reaffirm things God has already spoken over a person, encouraging them to continue on the path before them, and can give hope as they wait or work toward the purposes God has placed on their lives. God can also use this as an opportunity to speak His heart and love over the individual.

3. Comfort: This word can comfort, console, or encourage. The key is it does these things with great gentleness. Comfort is never harsh or abrasive, especially if the person receiving is already in a delicate place emotionally and spiritually. Paul is speaking in 1 Corinthians 14:3 of the still, small voice that speaks quietly, peacefully into the ear of the Church, particularly during times of stress or persecution. How kind God is that He chooses to speak comfort

over His children when we are going through
trials.

Let's dive a little deeper into these three points.

Edification for an individual will often adjust their direction or actions to be more in-line with the Word of God or an
impending change in their life. It will alert them to upcoming
events or a shift in direction. It is often a "get ready" kind of
word. A prophetic word that is corrective in nature should
be given in a closed session to the church leadership before it
is released to the congregation. Why should we do this? The
church leadership is anointed to shepherd the flock, and if
there is a word that impacts the flock, it needs to go to those
who watch over the sheep.

On occasion, the enemy will try to sneak into services
through prophecies (Matthew 7:15, 22–23; 1 Timothy 4:1–2).
One leader told me of a prophecy he had heard about where
one of the worship leaders started speaking from the demonic
and said, "I hate it when you praise the Lord, for I cannot do
my work in your midst." It is so important that prophetic
words (that might be directional for the congregations) pass
through the shepherds first. (I might add a proviso here that
when I have preached many years for a congregation, there
are times when there are somewhat directional prophecies
that come spontaneously and the leadership has given me
latitude to share. One such word, for instance, was about
breaking ground immediately for a new building, and God

would provide the funds if that was done. The pastor jumped up and said, "Let's do it now! Who has a shovel?" One was found in the back of someone's truck, and we marched out and "broke ground" right then and there. The money did come supernaturally after that to build a building. Money, I might add, that they had been trying to raise for a number of years.)

The Greek word for "encouragement" in 1 Corinthians 14:3 is *paraklesi[s]*, which comes from the same root as the special term "Paraclete," which is the term Jesus used in John's gospel to refer to the Holy Spirit. A word from God that is meant to encourage will remind us that we are not alone, God is in control, and all His promises are true.

Several years ago, I was diagnosed with a grapefruit-sized tumor and was very discouraged. The doctors were not sure if it was cancerous. However, right before this happened, I had been given an unusual Scripture verse of encouragement that did not feel like it applied to my life at the time. In fact, it was a little disturbing. The verse was Revelation 2:10:

> Do not fear any of those things which you are about to suffer. Indeed, the devil is about to throw some of you into prison, that you may be tested, and you will have tribulation ten days. Be faithful until death, and I will give you the crown of life.

Now faced with a tumor, I did not know if the Lord was telling me I would be tested for ten days and then to "be faithful until . . ." (I didn't prefer to think about the rest). Then I read where it said the devil was about to do his work, and so I stood firm on the Word of God and prayed for healing. I asked my doctor if I could postpone my surgery while I received prayer. My husband and a few others anointed me with oil, prayed over me, and ten days after asking to postpone the surgery, I received the news my tumor was completely gone. Not only was it gone, but there was no sign of stress on the other organs. That encouraging word from Revelation was given to me before I knew I was sick to encourage me through my time of trial.

A quick note regarding healing prophecies. For those suffering from serious illness or terminal medical conditions, words of encouragement or comfort can feel like fresh water in the desert. However, it is so important that both the person giving and receiving the word really press into what God is saying.

As a youth, I was witnessing at The Green Gate, a Christian club, when a drunk man staggered in to try to get some food. He looked at me in a bleary-eyed way and said, "Jesus, oh I once knew Jesus. In fact, I was a healer for Him. One day, I told a man not to take his three-year-old daughter to the doctor because God was going to heal her—and she died!" With a deep sigh of grief, he moaned, "I'll never forgive myself for that little girl's death." After talking for several hours, he was finally able to receive God's forgiveness and cried like a little baby as he was reunited with His Lord.

When prophesying over someone who has a serious illness or terminal medical condition, if you believe you have received a word for them regarding healing, it is important that you discern *how* the Lord wants to heal that person. Prophecies around healing can be presumptive rather than redemptive, and some suffering believers have taken a prophetic word and abandoned all medical treatment because they did not ask *how* God wanted to heal them. God can and has healed people supernaturally. He does that again and again throughout the Bible. He also utilizes medicine and modern treatments to achieve His healing purpose. Conveying to an ill person that "God is going to heal you" requires that you ask God how. He may already be using people and science to do just that.

"Comfort" in 1 Corinthians 14:3 is the word *paramuthia*, which according to Clifford Hill means "to exercise a gentle influence by speaking words of comfort, consolation, or encouragement."[1] The Lord knows the hearts of His children, which is why He often speaks to us in specific, personal ways. He wants us to know we are heard, seen, and known. This can give so much comfort.

One evening, I was ministering in Canada, and I kept hearing the name Albert again and again. The unusual part was I sensed Albert was the relative of some people attending the conference. The relatives were not sure if Albert was in heaven, and the Lord wanted to put them at rest, to comfort them. The prophecy went something like this: "There is someone here who had a relative named Albert, and the Lord wants you to know that he is in heaven." Later, a lady came up to me with a glowing face and said, "I was here tonight with my sister, and we were so blessed by the word you gave about Albert. Albert was our dad, and we never knew whether or not he was a Christian when he died. Tonight, we have been given great reassurance and peace."

APPLICATION

Think back to a time when you clearly heard God speaking to you through a prophetic word or speaking to you directly. Get a piece of paper and write out what you received with as much detail as you can recall. If you have a recording of the word, great! Listen to it and write out the words.

Now, ask yourself the following questions:

- Was this a redemptive word or a rebuke?
- When I received this, what was going on in my life? How was my heart responding to my circumstances before I received this word?
- After receiving this word, what did I feel and what did I do?
- Would I describe this word as edifying, encouraging, or comforting?

- What did I sense about God's heart toward me in that moment? What did that word teach me about His character?

Take a moment to thank the Lord for how He loves you, and how intimately He knows you. Thank Him for His voice speaking over you and ask what it is He has for you in this season.

3

Preparing to Hear God's Voice

Years ago, my church was conducting our big annual conference, and we were excited about the prospect of having a speaker whom I will call Reverend Simpson. He had given several accurate prophecies to us in the past, but for some reason, that night I felt uneasy. I couldn't put my finger on it, but something wasn't right. I began to talk to the Lord about how I felt, and from inside my heart came the words, *"Caution. This man has some severe personal problems. Watch and pray."*

At this point, Reverend Simpson came into the ballroom. He wore a business suit, and was tall and thin with deep-set eyes, gaunt-looking cheekbones, and long bony fingers. Instead of subsiding, the sense of something being wrong with this man increased dramatically. As he came up on the platform, I began to earnestly pray without uttering a sound. I then quietly said, "Satan, I bind you in the name of Jesus from giving a false word to this assembly through this man." It was impossible for him to physically hear what I whispered under my breath. So I was shocked when Reverend Simpson suddenly came and stood right in front of me on the platform, facing the audience. He started gesturing wildly with his hands and began stepping backward. Each step he took forced me to take a step back until I was literally up against the wall.

He then jumped off the platform, looking very confused. He looked around and then called the daughter of one of our leaders to the front to "prophesy" over her. I was shocked as he apparently touched her bosom by accident, then grabbed her by her ears and pinched her so hard she bled. By this time, I was upset and earnestly praying for this to stop—or I was going to stop it myself. Reverend Simpson gazed at the audience, muttered something about there not being any true prophets in our midst, and took off out of the room.

What happened here? We had previously been blessed by Reverend Simpson's ministry, how could things have taken such a strange and disturbing turn? I surmise several things could have happened:

- He had some sin issues that he had been able to keep hidden up to this time.

- Pride in the power of his ministry might have entered into his life. His comment about "no true prophets in our midst" seemed to indicate that he believed he was *the* true prophet.

- There is a possibility he had some sort of emotional breakdown that allowed the "beasts in the basement" of his sin issues to become uncontrollable for him.

In probing into the situation later, it appeared that he did not have much spiritual accountability in his life.

Unfortunately, this story is not an unusual or isolated one. Some weird people are attracted to the prophetic movement in the Church. This is a shame because there are many more genuine, balanced prophetic leaders than there are flaky ones. Those who have severe emotional and personal problems have caused real damage to the Body of Christ and have created a serious backlash against others who prophesy.

Although this damage may occur, the Bible is clear about the need to be able to receive the prophetic gifts in our midst. First Thessalonians 5:19–20 puts it this way: "Do not quench the Spirit. Do not despise prophecies." God exhorts us not to devalue prophetic revelation nor turn away from inspired instruction, exhortation, or warning.

In addition, people emerging with the gift of prophecy are often squelched. The Holy Spirit is then quenched and grieved because of a lack of basic understanding of how prophecy should function in the Church. Training is needed. And just as a toddler has many falls before he or she can walk well, the prophetic person in training will also stumble. The training of a prophetic person can at times seem quite severe, but training is necessary.

Character Training

Let's discuss some of the inner training God conducts on the prophetic person who may or may not one day be a prophet or prophetess. I personally believe many of these principles can be applied to all believers as they seek to grow in the Lord. It does stand to reason that the training of leaders who stand before thousands will be more intense than those who are not in such a visible ministry.

It is critical to note that although someone may operate in a powerful way with the gift of prophecy, it does not necessarily mean he or she has character enough to be in a visible ministry. As the apostle Paul said, "And I, brethren, could not speak to you as to spiritual people but as to carnal, as to babes in Christ . . . for you are still carnal" (1 Corinthians 3:1, 3).

Once someone is put into a place of visible ministry, every stronghold within that person often hatches. It is imperative that they receive proper mentorship and accountability, or they can easily fall into shame. Strong leadership is critical in the life of a growing prophet. This is why it is wise, both for those God is raising up for service and for those who are training them, to allow God to deal with major character flaws while these people are less visible.

Intrinsic to the nature of those in various kinds of ministries (such as the pastor, teacher, and evangelist) are certain weaknesses or strongholds. The same is true of prophets. Some of these problems, I believe, God allows in order to keep us totally reliant on Him.

Walk in Integrity

What does it mean for a child of God, much less a prophet of God, to walk in integrity? If the Lord is going to trust His words to specific people to speak, they must first be faithful in giving their word. It doesn't matter if you are interceding in private for your entire ministry or if you are operating in your gifting in the public eye, your integrity matters.

Here are a few ways that you can practice integrity in your walk:

1. Don't exaggerate. Speak what the Lord says and go no further than that. You do not need to make a word from God more exciting, fruitful, or dramatic than it actually is. In the same vein, do not downplay what you are hearing either. Share what you are hearing and trust the Lord to make the rest clear.

2. Be on time for commitments. Failing to arrive on time or allowing something to spill over into another

scheduled commitment can cause frustration in the people you are serving. This is an issue of learning how to properly order and organize your own life.

3. Keep your word. If people can't trust you to keep a promise, how can they trust you to have a prophecy from God? With busy lives and schedules, ask God to help you remember any commitments you have made, or leave yourself notes.

4. Handle money properly. Pay your bills on time, control your use of credit, and do not live beyond your means. Also, it is *so* important that prophetic leaders do not solicit funds as a prerequisite for giving a prophetic word from God. The gift of prophecy cannot be bought or sold. If you fall into that kind of behavior, you can fall into divination as did Balaam the seer in Numbers 22–24, and a former sorcerer named Simon in Acts 8:18–23.

5. Speak the pure word from God. It is possible for the prophetic word to be "tainted," which means that only part of what the prophet says is coming from God. Part of that tainting can come through the generational sins or occult activity in the life of the prophet.

Cleaning House: Generational Sins and Iniquities

You shall not worship them [idols] or serve them; for I, the LORD your God, am a jealous God, visiting the iniquity of the fathers on the children, and on the third and fourth generations of those who hate Me, but showing loving-kindness to thousands, to those who love me and keep My commandments.

Deuteronomy 5:9–10 NASB1995

As the years have gone by in my life and ministry, I have been puzzled by some of the areas with which I have struggled. Certain issues that I knew I had not personally been involved with would crop up and seemed to pull me in a strong way. While I looked for answers, it seemed that Scripture passages concerning generational sin leaped out at me in my studies. One of those passages was Deuteronomy 5:9–10 (above).

What are generational sins?

The phrase "generational sin" has grown in popularity over the past decade, as people with a background in the church will attribute any roadblock in their lives to a generational curse. You may even see motivational speakers outside of the Christian faith declare that you too can break off generational curses and strongholds and throw off the things holding you back. However, this isn't a fad phrase or a way to move further in life than your parents did. Generational sins are scriptural. The sins, weaknesses, and tendencies toward certain sins exhibited by a person's parents will be passed on (the Hebrew word is *pagad*, meaning "visit" or "appoint") to the children. Even people who come from Christian families and are devoted believers, filled with the Holy Spirit, can be visited by these weaknesses and tendencies.

Here is an example. A pregnant woman goes for an X-ray, and the unborn child becomes deformed by the X-ray. The unborn child didn't order the X-ray and is entirely a victim, but nonetheless is affected by the X-ray. Sin, like the X-ray, damages the generations. This is a powerful thought and should put the fear of the Lord in us before we enter into sin.

Sin vs. iniquity

In their book *A Woman's Guide to Breaking Bondages*, Quin Sherrer and Ruthanne Garlock state:

> The iniquity of the forefathers brings a curse upon the family line. This word *iniquity* does not mean individual sinful acts; it means "perverseness" and comes from a Hebrew root meaning "to be bent or crooked." The word implies a basic attitude of rebellion, plus the consequences that iniquity produces.[1]

Sin is basically the cause. Iniquity includes the effect. A parent can commit a sin such as occult involvement or sexual sin, and that produces a curse. The curse then causes a generational iniquity or weakness to pass down the family line. Just as venereal disease can produce physical deformity, so spiritual sin produces spiritual deformity in the generations.

How do we identify generational sins and iniquities?

If you are seeing evidence of iniquities in your life, ask God to reveal to you any generational sin issues in your family line that are producing these results. Not all hardships are the result of a generational sin or iniquity, but if you are seeing patterns of behavior or tendencies that are not in line with God's Word, and they exist in other members of your family, ask the Lord.

These are some examples of sins that later become generational:

1. Occult involvement and witchcraft. "Witchcraft is the power or practice of witches' sorcery; black magic."[2] Another definition could be anything that draws its power from any source other than God. This includes Ouija boards, astrology, tarot cards, water dowsers, and "psychic healers." There is no such thing as white or harmless magic; it is demonic and derives its power from Satan.

2. Secret societies. Involvement with societies such as Freemasonry, Eastern Star, and the Shriners allows demonic access to the generations. These groups require members to take oaths that are not of God and are not biblical. Do not be deceived by the fact that these groups are involved in good works and charitable

giving. They are still tied to demonic activity, and they open a door to the demonic in your bloodline.

3. Robbing and defrauding God. Do not neglect to give God back the portion that is due to Him. Malachi 3:8–9 says, "Will a man rob or defraud God? Yet you rob and defraud Me. But you say, 'In what way do we rob or defraud You?' *[You have withheld your] tithes and offerings.* You are cursed with the curse, for you are robbing Me, even this whole nation" (AMPC, emphasis added).

4. Bondages. Dean Sherman says a bondage involves a supernatural element. "If we continue in a habit of sin, we can develop a bondage. A bondage means there is a supernatural element to our problem. The enemy now has a grip on a function of our personality."[3] Bondages in the generations can pass down and become iniquities for later generations. Not all compulsions, addictions, or sin habits necessarily begin with our forefathers, but many do. Although you are encouraged to deal with today's issues and your own sin problems, it would be a mistake to discount the possibility that there are sins of the father playing a role.

How do we break free from generational sins?

It is crucial for all believers to be free of generational bondages and iniquities. It is absolutely critical for those who prophesy. The axe must be laid to the root of all pulls of the carnal flesh, as well as generational iniquities.

How do we do this? I have identified the following seven steps:

1. Identify specifically the sin of your forefathers (this includes foremothers).

2. Repent for the sin in a manner something like this: "Father God, I ask forgiveness for the sin of _____ (witchcraft, lust, or whatever you've specifically identified) and now repent for this sin to the third and fourth generations. I now renounce this sin and cut it off from myself and my seed and my seed's seed. By this prayer, I lay the axe to the root of my sin in Jesus' name, Amen."

3. Break the power of any curses that might have come as a result of the sin. A sample prayer could be: "Father God, according to Deuteronomy 28, idolatry brings a curse. I thank You for forgiving the sin of idolatry of money [for example]. I now break the curse of poverty in Jesus' name. Thank You for setting me, as well as my generation, free in Jesus' name. I now apply the blood of the Lamb in faith to my generation as well as those to come."

4. Command any fruit of these generational sins to wither up and die in your life and the lives of your children.

5. Ask the Lord to heal all negative effects of the generational iniquities in your life.

6. Identify the bondages and habits that have grown from these generational sins.

7. Take ownership of these bondages, habits, and addictions. Confess them to the Lord and ask Him to work in your carnal nature to renew your mind in these areas. You may need to seek help from someone to break the bondages. James 5:16 gives us a beautiful promise concerning confessing our sins or trespasses: "Confess your trespasses to one another, and pray for one another, that you may be healed. The effective, fervent prayer of a righteous man avails much."

Prophetic people need to have the fear of the Lord operating in their lives much more than others do. It is crucial that they be whole people. Whatever issues need to be dealt with, both past and present (selfishness, pride, brokenness from family of origin, and so on) need to be brought under God's divine searchlight. The fire of God will purge and cleanse us as we allow the Holy Spirit to deal with bitterness and bring us to the place where we are vessels of honor in the service of the King.

APPLICATION

Begin with prayer, asking the Lord to make you aware of any places of habits, weakness, or iniquities in your life. You may be surprised at what He highlights. Or perhaps you are already aware of some patterns that need to go. Let Him really root around and bring the core issues to light.

Once you have identified the issue, ask if this is something that also exists in other family members. Do you feel drawn to certain things that you can't seem to shake? The issue may not be generational, but it still needs to be repented of and turned from. If you do believe it is a generational sin, go back to the seven steps in the last section. It may be helpful to have a trusted prayer partner walk through them with you.

Finally, ask yourself if there are areas you can grow in. Are you being asked to grow in your prayer life? Set a time in your day where you know you can focus on prayer. Is the Lord calling you outside of your bubble and into community? Begin searching for ways to do that.

4

Is There a Protocol
for Prophesying?

Several years ago, I was attending a prayer meeting in the Los Angeles area that was organized to specifically intercede for the city. The event was attended by renowned and respected pastors, evangelic leaders, and charismatic and Pentecostal voices. There was such a feeling of unity, and we could sense the sweetness of the Holy Spirit's presence as we prayed and worshiped together.

Suddenly, a man with wild-looking eyes began yelling from the back of the church and broke our peaceful worship. His voice and body language expressed intense anger, and legalism oozed from his words as he proclaimed something to the effect of "Thus sayeth the Lord, 'Woe to the shepherds who build fancy homes for themselves and do not take care of My people. They do not feed the poor and the homeless, nor see the hurting.'"

One of the leaders spoke up with authority and graciousness. "Sir, would you please restrain yourself. According to the Word, the spirit of the prophet is subject to the prophet. You can control that. You are out of order." The man was ushered out of the meeting, continuing to yell as he went out. The leaders apologized for what had occurred, and they tried to put the shards of the meeting back together.

Later in the meeting, an evangelic leader stood and began to pray. His voice broke as he uttered his petition to the Lord. "Lord God," he said, "we have not always noticed the needs of others in our busyness of service. Father, help us to be sensitive to others' needs." The sound of soft weeping filled the room. I realized this was the correct word the Lord wanted to speak over His people. He did not want the busy leaders to be "beat up" for their oversights by a word of condemnation. He simply wanted to remind them they needed to refocus on their priorities. They required a gentle reminder, not a stern rebuke. The presumptuous intruder had indeed heard something from God but interpreted it through a religious filter.

It is so important to remember that God is a God of order (1 Corinthians 14:33). The opposite of order is disorder and confusion. When we establish order and protocols in the prophetic ministry, it gives a prophetic word the structure to have a powerful, catalyzing influence on the church. If we minister incorrectly and in a state of disorder or confusion, it can cause enormous confusion and damage to the body. Protocols are not legalism; they are structure that gives the Spirit room to move without our flesh jumping in the way.

One dictionary definition of "protocol" states: "in diplomacy, protocol is the ceremonial forms and courtesies that are established as proper and correct in official intercourse between heads of states and their ministers."[1] How perfectly that fits with the way God's Kingdom functions! The spiritual Kingdom carries on its affairs through the local church and through delegated authority, and the exchange must be proper and correct.

Defining Authority

To understand order, it is imperative to grasp the concept of spiritual authority. Without proper spiritual authority, anarchy will occur, and that can lead to a leadership vacuum (among other things). When a leadership vacuum occurs, someone will fill the void. That could be a person acting in their flesh, or it could be a person sent by Satan to disrupt.

In the book *Spiritual Authority*, based on his 1948 speech, Watchman Nee draws the connection between will and authority. "Before [Jesus] knew the will of God, the cup and God's will were two separate things; and after He knew it was of God, however, the cup and God's will merged into one. Will represents authority. Therefore, to know God's will and to obey it is to be subject to authority."[2]

> Obey your spiritual leaders and submit to them [continually recognizing their authority over you], for they are constantly keeping watch over your souls and guarding your spiritual welfare, as men who will have to render an account [of their trust]. [Do your part to] let them do this with gladness and not with sighing and groaning, for that would not be profitable to you [either].
>
> Hebrews 13:17 AMPC

What Does Submission Look Like?

How do we live out Hebrews 13:17 and submit to our spiritual leaders in obedience? There is protection in submitting to a local assembly, whether it is the kind of covering you desire or not. My husband, Mike, and I are blessed to attend a church that believes in the gifts of the Holy Spirit flowing freely. They give honor to the office of the prophets. When I preach or give the word of the Lord for our church, our pastor and his team judge the word, and then he leads prayer for twenty-one days using that word as well as words from other prophetic voices.

One year, I prophesied when the church was at 2,000 members, "This church will double in one year." My pastor went to his elders and trustees and asked, "If our church doubles, how many parking spaces do we need and what additional children's facilities do we need?" They began a capital campaign to build and prepare for the church to double in size. One year later, the church had doubled in size, and they opened the new space!

Mike and I have built that relationship with our pastor over time. When you "pay your dues" in submission, your pastor will learn to trust you, and you can have a powerful relationship with a leader who believes that God still speaks today. You can be a trusted voice and a prophetic intercessor, even if you don't have a pulpit ministry in your church.

Do I think you need to submit to everything your pastor says, regardless of what it may be? Of course not. I am greatly concerned about some churches that call themselves "prophetic churches" but exercise so much control over their members' lives that they are highly dysfunctional, controlling, and border on being a cult (or may already be one). You absolutely have the space to exercise discretion, hold things up to the light of the Scriptures, and ask questions. Just be sure that whatever you do is covered in love and respect for your leaders.

Submission to a delegated authority is not always easy because the authority figure placed over you may not be a person you would have selected. In learning to submit to delegated authority, personal pride issues may need to be addressed, especially when it comes to leadership and promotion within the church. God promotes on a basis different from the world, not necessarily according to physical ages or years in the Kingdom. Many times, learning to submit to authority figures you would not have chosen is a test for you.

David's submission to Saul is one of the greatest examples of submission to delegated authority in the Bible (1 Samuel 18–19, 24). Saul was extremely jealous of the attention David received after his victories in battle and became obsessed and suspicious of David. Even though Saul was trying to kill him, David kept his heart right, even spurning the opportunity to kill Saul. David had great authority because he understood authority. Saul had been placed over David, but was abusive in his authority, which left David in a quandary. Although David protected himself, he did not overtly attack the king because Saul had been appointed by God.

Spiritual Issues Prophets Face

Prophets are susceptible to attacks when they are operating in their gifting, learning their gifting, or in a position of leadership. Basically, they are always a target for the enemy. It is so easy for issues of pride, rejection, and bitterness to slip in through the cracks in our spirits, and these can have big effects on our ministries.

Here are some of the spiritual issues prophets often face:

Issues with submission

We have established that there is authority in the church. Where there is authority, there can be people who struggle with submission to that authority.

Submission to delegated authority: When you join a church, you make a covenant not only with the local body of Christ but also with God to obey that leadership. The leadership over the church also has a responsibility before God to keep watch over your soul. Any pastor who truly understands his role in the church will take his shepherding of the sheep very seriously. Many members do not fathom how this heavily weighs on their pastor, so it is painful for leaders to see their young prophetic people—or other church people—reject the counsel and wisdom they could be given through local church leadership.

Submission to the local church: Do not be a "lone ranger" prophetic minister. I cannot stress this enough. Even if you feel that "no one understands my gifting," you need to pray and search until you find the local church you need. You may have to move to another location to come into covenant relationship with a church in another city, but there is protection in being submitted to a local assembly, whether it is the kind of covering you desire or not. Satan loves to pick off the sheep who strike out on their own, away from the protection of a shepherd, and it is hard to grow without the accountability that comes from being in a church.

Promotion and submission: One of the hardest situations is when a leader who is younger than you or has been in the ministry a shorter time is brought into a position to which you must submit. This often exposes what I call an "elder brother" spirit (taken from the parable of the prodigal son in Luke 15). When the elder brother saw his younger brother receive a welcome fit for a king, he flew into a jealous fit. Jealousy and pride are ugly things, but remember: God promotes on a basis different from the world, not necessarily according to physical ages or years in the Kingdom. The good part about being criticized and passed over is that it tends to keep you humble and tender toward those whom others might look down upon.

Rejection and submission: Years ago, I was part of a church that did not understand the prophetic gifting (and frankly, neither did I at that time). Because of this, I did things out of order. I was also a woman in a church where women did not share from the pulpit. After some time serving at this church, I started to notice a chill developed in the air when I entered a room; something was wrong. So I went to the Lord, and He answered me: "*Cindy, they think you're practicing divination. Go speak to the associate pastor and his wife.*" Mike and I went and sat with the associate pastor and his wife, and they revealed that the senior pastor had indeed told his staff that I was practicing divination. He had laughed at the times I prophesied, and he had accused me of divination before other leaders in the area. I was crushed.

I went to the Lord in prayer, and I fully expected God to vindicate me by sending some fire from heaven down upon the pastor's head. Instead, the Lord said with compassion, "*Cindy, I'd like to use you more, but you're too sensitive.*" Leaders deal with rejection many, many times. If you can resist rejection and deal with it as it comes, you are better prepared for God to use you. I did not sound off against my pastor. Instead, we remained at that church until we were officially released later when it was time for our family to move on. Years passed, that pastor actually apologized to me, and we had the opportunity to minister together at a conference, which brought great healing.

Obedience and submission: There will be times in your ministry when God tells you to speak up, sit down, or He hands the microphone to another person at a meeting you believed you were called to lead. On one occasion, I had been invited to be one of the main speakers at an outdoor crusade. To say I was excited would be minimizing my feelings. I had prepared the message, sensed the anointing, and couldn't wait for the night to come. I also was going to have to travel a long, long way to speak.

The afternoon of the meeting arrived, and the leader overseeing the outreach came to me. "Cindy, the pastors' committee feels I should preach tonight." The blood rushed to my head, and I headed to my room. Mike found me there, being very spiritual—I was crying my eyes out. He comforted me until I calmed down and got still before the Lord. All of a sudden, I understood that this was a test. I asked myself "Do I think I have to be the instrument of God for His people?" This speaker could certainly reach people I couldn't. I decided to pray that God would bless the preacher's message, and that as a result, many would come into the Kingdom of God. That night, the preacher gave an invitation, and people poured to the front with tears streaming down their faces. "Oh, thank You, God," I sighed. "You are so good. You knew just the right person to minister Your Word tonight for these people."

My friend, our glory doesn't matter. His does. Even if you are confused by what He is saying, obey Him and submit to what He is doing. God blesses obedience. It is better than sacrifice.

Abuse and submission: The balance between not submitting to abuse and keeping our attitude right can be delicate. When we have an adverse reaction to something a leader tells us, it is time to search our own hearts. We need to ask: "Am I reacting out of past hurts and wounds, or is this really abuse? Is this person really like Saul in his treatment of David?" The truth may not be evident at first, but may require a prayerful time of seeking the Lord.

In 1 Chronicles 16:22, we see, "Do not touch My anointed ones, and do My prophets no harm." This has wrongly been taken to mean that the people in the church cannot think for themselves or question anything a leader says. That is dysfunctional and not what the verse means. It does mean that even in the midst of our questioning, we need to keep our hearts right and not attack. If we unjustly come against a leader, God will protect and take care of the leader, and we will answer to the Lord for what we've done.

Issues with honor and authority

One little-understood concept in the Church today is that of honoring those in authority over us. We need to understand how to esteem and respect our leaders. We honor them not just as people, but also for the positions in which the Lord has put them. Even under great duress, Paul modeled an attitude of honor in Acts 23:1–5 when he was dragged before the Sanhedrin. He submitted in his spirit, not to his abusers but to the position they held. This is what David understood about Saul. He did not submit to the abuse—nor should we—but he kept his attitude right.

Years ago, a leader who was my age was greatly upset by something an older leader had done. He wrote a letter of correction and called to ask my advice about sending it. I thought a moment and said, "You know, if you send that letter, the person won't receive it from you. Besides, the Word says we are not to rebuke an elder. The person will chalk it off as criticism."

We determined that we should pray, and we agreed that someone who was a peer to the leader should speak to him, as he would be more apt to take correction from a peer.

Further, we asked God to soften the leader's heart to listen to the correction when it came. Now, this leader had hurt many people through the years by harsh words and insensitive remarks; I had received other calls from young leaders who were fed up with the treatment they had received from that leader. However, he was a wonderful Bible teacher, and we wanted to be sure that, at least in our hearts, we were right before God.

God remarkably answered our prayer that day. I later heard this person speak and share publicly how God had been dealing with his harshness and hardness of heart.

In some cases, respecting and honoring God's anointed can be a real challenge. Truly, some leaders can slip from a place of great anointing, and something happens to them that spoils it. This could be attributed to pride, deep personal tragedy, or a stronghold bubbling to the surface. The temptation of a young leader is to want to rebuke the older leader, who they believe has become like King Saul, but that is not a biblical response. First Timothy 5:1 says, "Do not rebuke an older man, but exhort him as a father." The King James Version uses the word "elder" for "older man." The connotation of "do not rebuke" is to not upbraid or chastise. Too often, we see young leaders with wounds (often legitimate) who respond from a place of hurt or rejection, and accusations and names are thrown around. A leader who has brought thousands to Christ can suddenly be accused of a Jezebel spirit or a Saul spirit. This can be devastating.

Let me define a few of these "spirits" that we refer to in our church vernacular. Perhaps if we have a better understanding of what they actually mean, we will be more careful before using these titles on our fellow brothers and sisters.

The Saul spirit: Saul was jealous, controlling, manipulative, and a potential murderer. I have seen many pastors incorrectly accused of having a Saul spirit, when they were actually just *in process*, like you and me. If you are struggling with your leadership, be like David and refuse to touch God's anointed. Refuse to speak behind the pastor's back. Remember, you will be responsible to God for your actions and words. If you are under the thumb of a Saul and he is hurling javelins at you, seek the Lord regarding whether you should go or stay. If you are called to leave, do everything you can to leave correctly; don't just dart off without a word.

The Jezebel spirit: Christians throw this name around so glibly, and I don't believe they realize what they are doing. Some people can certainly become Jezebels, but this is a serious accusation. Revelation 2:20 describes Jezebel as one who calls herself a prophetess, who led God's people to worship false gods, which included cult prostitution. Jezebel is a controller, a deceiver; she is immoral, and has a destroying and murderous spirit. We should be very careful before branding any strong leader with that horrible woman's name. We need to have the fear of the Lord on our lives before we accuse anyone of having a Jezebel spirit, and not simply because we do not agree with them or do not like their treatment of us.

The Absalom spirit: Absalom tried to take over his father David's kingdom. This attitude of rebellion or betrayal, however, not only affects intercessors, but also young prophetic people. Young people training in the prophetic are highly susceptible to becoming like Absalom. Here are some reasons for this, and the problems it causes:

- Prophetic people tend to discern the faults and vulnerabilities in other leaders. This is because the Lord wants them to grow in the area of intercessory prayer.

- Prophetic people often try to give corrective words with incorrect protocol. When the correction isn't received or acted upon in a fashion or with the timetable they prefer, they become bitter. They don't understand that they may have discerned accurately but were wrong in their delivery.

- Bitter young prophetic leaders tend to "spout off" or tell others what they see in the church or among the leadership. This can cause a critical spirit to rise up against the leaders. Critical people in the church can then be like birds of a feather, flocking together. It's amazing how quickly critical clusters can form in a church because a few young leaders are speaking in bitterness.

- Deception can easily enter at this point. Such prophets can become seduced into believing they know better than others or that they should be the pastor themselves. Sometimes, they can claim they know who should be the pastor instead of the current one.
- Such deception and dissension can lead to full-blown mutiny. Though the prophetic person may have discovered a true problem at first, he or she can handle it in such a wrong way that they become like Absalom, full of a rebellious spirit.

While we are not denying that there can be abuses in leadership, and some older leaders can be very hurtful, doing more damage than good at times, the way you handle the situation is critical.

A word of caution to leaders with young prophetic people under your leadership: Try to listen to your young leaders and see past their arrogance or their incorrect delivery of a word. Then, tenderly share with them the part of the prophecy you believe is accurate (if any). Find some way to affirm them and gently give them instruction about the correct protocol for the delivery of a prophecy to eldership.

One final admonishment on this topic, to the young leaders: Remember, love covers a multitude of sins (1 Peter 4:8). Treat older leaders as you would want to be treated in similar seasons of your life.

Issues with handling conflict

If a conflict arises or if there is a disagreement to be settled, Matthew 18:15–17 gives us a clear biblical model on this subject: "Moreover, if your brother sins against you, go and tell him his fault between you and him alone. If he hears you, you have gained your brother" (v. 15).

In the church, the first step is often skipped: We tell everyone else about the problem without approaching the one with whom we have a disagreement. Before you go to someone regarding an offense, pray and ask the Lord to soften both your hearts. Seek the Lord for the power of the Holy Spirit to be in the midst of the meeting. You might use the authority of binding to stop Satan from interfering with the meeting or causing rejection to enter into the process (Matthew 12:29; 16:18–19; Luke 10:17–19).

"But if he will not hear, take with you one or two more, that 'by the mouth of two or three witnesses every word may be established'" (Matthew 18:16). This is the second step. If you have tried to talk it out and have not been successful, ask a mediator or two to join you. Ask the Lord for the correct timing—when the person you are confronting can emotionally take the intensity of such a meeting.

We hope most offenses will never get to step three: "And if he refuses to hear them, tell it to the church. But if he refuses even to hear the church, let him be to you like a heathen and a tax collector" (v. 17). Some churches have jumped right to this step without ever following the proper protocols and have publicly excommunicated people without giving them a chance to bring in neutral mediators. Churches must be careful about what they say to large groups regarding people who have fallen into sin. After a person repents and changes, the comment can follow him or her (and their family) for the rest of the person's life. It is better to deal with these situations in private.

Protocols

If you believe you have received a word from the Lord, and He is asking you to share it, there are a few things you will need to understand first.

We can't be prepared for every situation. However, these are the protocols that I believe are in line with Scripture and provide a structure for sharing a word from the Lord in a manner that is orderly and beneficial.

Protocols for delivering prophetic words

Not only are there clear biblical guidelines for corporate prophecy, but each church and group also seem to have their own rules, cultures, and boundaries. It is entirely possible for you to bump against some unwritten code within a church and feel clueless about why people become upset after you give a prophetic word. Some leaders have a certain set of ethics themselves, and they just assume after a length of time that everyone knows those ethics.

Sharing a personal prophecy with leaders: If you have established credibility as a prophetic voice with the church or person whom you feel the word is for, you need to share it with someone who can judge it for you—someone whose confidentiality you trust. If you have not established credibility in your local church, the protocol would be to ask one of the leaders in your church to judge the prophetic word. Present it to someone in leadership who knows how to judge prophetic words and present it as "I received this while I was in prayer for you. Would you look it over?" Once you have delivered the word, leave it to the Lord to bring it to pass if it was indeed from Him.

Sharing a prophecy in the local church: As I've traveled to various nations and have worked with a spectrum of churches and organizations, I have found that not only do they follow biblical guidelines for prophesying, but they also have a culture of their own. If you are new to a church, it is best to clearly understand its policy and beliefs before you launch out. There are churches that only allow a few people to give prophetic words (this is usually because of some kind of past abuse by someone moving in the gift of prophecy). However, when the gifts are taught properly from the pulpits by pastors or explained in small groups, I have rarely seen them misused in a public setting. Some churches allow for the free expression of gifts. Is one method better than the other? I believe the biblical method is best (1 Corinthians 12 and 14). It is always wise to remain open to better ways of honing the use of the prophetic gift in the church.

Sharing corporate prophecy: If a prophecy is for the church congregation, and you receive it before the service, write it down and give it to an elder you trust. If what you received is more than a simple prophecy, and it has a forthtelling element or direction for the church body, you need to have it judged and approved before you give it to the congregation. If the prophecy is accurate, the elders will be able to determine when it should be given, and they will ask you to hold it until the proper time in the church service. Breaking spiritual protocol and blurting out a word (or a corrective word) can lead to great confusion within the church body.

Sharing at a conference: Prophetic words given at a church conference for the church's own people will usually follow the guidelines of the church itself. If the church is opening the conference to people from other churches and still wants to release the prophetic gifts during the worship services, it is appropriate to give some kind of explanation to those visiting to avoid confusion. Conferences designed to promote unity should probably require that prophecies given by attendees be written down and given to one of the conference leaders. In this way, the leaders can still harvest or glean from what God is saying to the whole group without exercising public prophecy. Conferences that range in attendance from four thousand and greater might consider putting together a prophetic team for practical reasons.

Protocols for tongues and interpretation

Tongues and interpretation can be sensitive areas, and I've considered the best way to explain protocol regarding these two subjects. I believe there are three perspectives concerning tongues and interpretation:

1. Cessationist: The belief that tongues ceased with the last apostle. The spiritual protocol for those who attend a church holding a cessationist view is that it is out of order to give a prophecy using tongues and interpretation. It would produce confusion. This perspective is also true for mixed gatherings that are promoting unity. Tongues is a hot issue that is much debated, and so it does not edify the Body of Christ at large in mixed meetings.

2. Third Wave: This is the belief that tongues is a gift of the Spirit given to some of the Body of Christ. Peter Wagner is one of the major leaders of the third-wave movement. This is his definition of the gift of tongues and of interpretation: "The gift of tongues is the special ability that God gives to certain members of the Body of Christ (A) to speak to God in a language they have never learned, and/or (B) to

receive and communicate an immediate message of God to His people through a divinely-anointed utterance in a language they have never learned."[3]

3. Charismatic or Pentecostal: Tongues are available through the empowering of the Holy Spirit to every believer. A private devotional tongue is given to every Christian, as found in Acts 2, and the ability to give public tongues and interpretation is found in 1 Corinthians 12:10 and 14:5.

   a. The first type, a private devotional tongue, has been described as the man or woman speaking to God through the power of the Holy Spirit.

   b. The second type, which is given publicly, is God speaking through a man or woman to His people.

Leaders need to be aware of their responsibilities regarding interpretation or translation whenever a tongue is given and no one else can interpret. The leader or one of the other leaders of the meeting should be prepared to ask God to give an interpretation. On the other hand, leaders should not assume they are the ones who always have to, or should, interpret. God might want to use others. I have found that when leaders always interpret the word, it loses its freshness because God wants to use the whole Body of Christ to speak, not just the church leadership (1 Corinthians 14:26). If only the leaders interpret, it can create a spiritual elitist mentality both in the leaders and in the people.

Here are a few additional things to note regarding tongues:

- Sometimes the word given in tongues may be short, but the interpretation can seem lengthy.

- Sometimes it is the reverse. The word in tongues will seem long but have a brief interpretation.

- I have seen instances when a person who has a prophecy for the service will tack it on to a tongue as an interpretation. However, it may not be the correct interpretation at all, but rather a separate prophecy. Sometimes, if it is appropriate and will not destroy the momentum of what God is doing in a service, I will mention that I feel the prophecy was from the Lord, but not the interpretation of the tongue. I will then ask the person with the interpretation to please give it.

- At times, the tongue is simply an adoration to God, but giving the adoration so lifts up the person or another hearer that it prompts a prophetic word to be given. This could also be a reason a person may give a long tongue and the interpretation seems short or vice versa. It could be that when the tongue is given from God to the congregation, a translation will follow, but when it is simply adoration, an interpretation will be given.

- If a tongue that is simply adoration to God is given, God at times has given me the exact translation of the adoration. I have found that God, through the Holy Spirit, will touch a person to express the corporate feelings the church is experiencing at that moment, and it releases a greater level of adoration through the whole body.

- It is possible for a tongue not to be of the Lord at all. Instead of releasing peace in the meeting, it produces unrest and agitation. The tongue might be strident, angry, or harsh, and that needs correction publicly from the leader in charge.

APPLICATION

Have there been times when you have either struggled with submission to an authority in your church, or you have seen blatant abuse? Grab your journal and write a few lines about that experience.

- What was the spark that ignited the issue?
- When you first knew there was a problem, who did you go to? How was it handled?
- Are there any lingering feelings you are carrying that need to be released to God?

Now, I encourage you to ask the Lord if there is anything in this situation that you need to confess. If there is bitterness, unforgiveness, or anything else that snuck in as a result of the issue, that needs to be dealt with before the Lord. Even if the offense was completely the fault of the leader, your heart is your responsibility.

On the issue of prophecy and tongues, what has been your experience in church with the use of tongues? What did that section of this chapter stir up in you? How have you seen prophecies given in the past in your church? If you have never seen a prophetic word given, I would encourage you to go to your church leaders and just inquire what the church's stance on receiving and delivering words happens to be.

— 5 —

Releasing the Prophetic Gift

I always encourage people to ask the Lord to allow them to prophesy. Even if they don't have the gift, the Lord may use them occasionally. The Bible exhorts us to earnestly desire to prophesy (1 Corinthians 14:39). Many times, when the Holy Spirit is moving in a meeting, almost anyone who is prophetic can prophesy. This doesn't mean they are to do so, but they need to be willing and available to the Lord if He should desire it.

One critical factor for anyone who is going to be used by the Lord to prophesy is to make sure his or her prayer life and time in the Scripture stays in balance. You can always tell a prophetic person who spends time steeped in God's Word; there is a richness to the prophetic gift that is liberally enhanced with Scripture. This is also a great safeguard against deception.

At times, the Holy Spirit will manifest through prophecy in a meeting. When this occurs, many prophecies will be spoken, and many who do not usually prophesy will be able to do so. It sometimes seems like a river of prophecy is flowing through the gathering as one person picks up where the last person left off.

One of the ways I frequently receive a prophetic word is I open my mouth and start to speak, trusting the Lord to give me His words. I realize that for beginners, this could be really scary. Other times, I receive just a few words or a complete sentence. If I am faithful with the little portion I have, more of the prophecy comes to me through the inspiration of the Holy Spirit as I go along.

Many times, when I have given a word, I have experienced trepidation afterward. When I first began to prophesy to well-known leaders, I would struggle to give the word, and then if they didn't give me feedback about its accuracy, I would struggle after I gave it. This is partially because of the stronghold I had to deal with concerning fear of other people.

Several times, I would give a word and for years not know how much the word had changed the lives of the people I gave it to. Although it is true that leaders can be overwhelmed by people who think they have heard from God on their behalf, you may be the one voice they need to hear. As long as you follow the biblical protocol, I would encourage you to go ahead and share what you are hearing. It may be just what that leader is waiting to hear to confirm something God is saying to him or her.

When Do I Release a Word?

Let's talk about timing. There have been instances when I have felt the anointing so strongly it was like fire burning in my bones, but I waited a year to give that prophecy. Sometimes, prophecies are not meant to be given out loud, but are meant to be used for intercessory prayer.

So how do you know if and when to prophesy?

- Remember, you can trust the Holy Spirit to give you a deep sense of His presence and peace.
- Ask "Is this a prophetic word God is speaking to me personally, or is it to be shared with everyone?" Sometimes it can be for both.
- Ask an elder what he or she thinks of what you are hearing and if the timing is right.

Once you have a sense of who it is for, and if an elder affirms the timing and message is right for the moment, here are a few confirming signs to help you know whether a prophecy is for that given church service:

- It will be in the same flow as what God is doing with the whole service. It will be similar in nature (gentle and comforting or strong and bold).

- The leaders will confirm the timing is right and find a place for it to flow into the service. If you are not sure about the timing, write the word down and share it with the pastor, so they can determine if the timing is now or if it is for later in the service.

- If the word is correctional, unless I am a recognized prophet in the local church, I do not give it publicly. Correctional words need to be submitted to the leadership for them to pray over and judge.

Prophesying during a church service

In general, I avoid prophesying in a church I am just visiting. However, sometimes the Lord gives me a word for that church. If the word is a true one, He always opens a door for me to give it. If you are visiting a church and feel you have a prophecy, this is what you might do:

- Ask an usher if you can speak to the elder or leader who judges the prophetic words given to the church. It is often good to write it down so he or she can read it rather than trying to talk to the person in the middle of the service.

- Pray for favor, and then release the giving of the word back to the Lord. He might use someone who is already recognized in that local body to speak the word.

- Wait and trust the Lord and the leadership in the church to discern if and when the prophecy should be given.

Private vs. corporate settings

As I shared before, if the word is for the corporate church service, it should fit with the flow of that service and amplify what God is already saying and doing. Pray and ask the Lord how to link what He is giving you with the worship that has preceded it. The exception to this would be when the service is going in a totally different direction from where the Holy Spirit wishes it to go, and the prophecy is a word from God to push the meeting back on track. The prophetic word can also be used by the Lord to break spiritual bondages and oppression (Psalm 107:20). If this is the case, heaviness of spirit is often lifted, and a time of rejoicing in God takes the place of sadness.

Sometimes, the word you receive may actually be for a person rather than the congregation. If this is the case and you are new at prophesying, have the word judged by someone you respect, rather than blurting it out. I will always talk to the pastor about a word I have for someone in his congregation to see whether he feels it should be given at that time. Always preface such prophetic words by saying something like "I am sensing this" or "Could it be that God wants to do this in your life?"

Prophesying online

With the advent of the internet, and millions of people now walking through life with instant access to video and streaming services on their smartphones, new challenges can emerge. Anyone with a phone can jump onto the internet, claiming to be a prophet, and deliver a supposed word from God. It goes without saying that while there are legitimate, true prophets using the internet as a powerful platform to share what God is revealing, the lack of structure and protocols can easily create an open door for the enemy to manipulate and deceive.

I would encourage you to use the same principles that are used to judge an in-person prophetic word when evaluating a word given on the internet. Here are some of the standards we need to utilize:

- Words need to be evaluated against the Scriptures.
- If it is in direct contrast to the character of God and the Bible, it is not a word from God.
- If you are giving the word, I highly recommend that you submit the word you received to those in authority over you so they can test and judge the word. If you are not submitted to a local church, you need to be. Remember: no lone rangers.
- If you are "receiving" the word (you are watching the video or reading a social media post), check what

you are hearing against the Scriptures and nature of God. Also consider the fruit of the person who is speaking. What does their life and ministry look like? Is it full of the fruit of the Spirit? Are they connected to a church and therefore have godly authority and accountability over them? Also check *your* heart and see if you are seeking out voices on the internet that confirm what you are hoping to hear, instead of listening openly for what God is saying at this point in time.

The web can be used to reach so many people with the word of God. However, where there are not church protocols, we can still use order and structure to ensure the word of God is not misused to stir up chaos, deception, and confusion.

What Happens If the Word Isn't 100 Percent Accurate?

When we read the Scriptures, we often see references to false prophets who were corrupting the people of Israel and leading them away from worship of the one true God. The Lord fiercely condemns these false prophets, and we see many met with very grim ends.

As you are leaning into the prophetic gift, the fear of operating as a false prophet is a very normal one that surfaces. Actually, most of the people I know who are prophets have been called false prophets at some point in their ministry.

However, there are definitive characteristics that mark a false prophet; making a mistake or misinterpreting something you hear from the Lord is not one of those characteristics.

The prophet Nathan wasn't labeled a false prophet even though he missed the prophecy at first in telling David he could build the Temple (2 Samuel 7:3). Jonah wasn't killed because his prophecy didn't come to pass about the destruction of Nineveh (Jonah 3:4, 10). When you are first learning to hear from the Lord and operate in your prophetic gifting, you will make mistakes. That does not make you a false prophet. I also want to caution you to please be extremely careful if you are proclaiming another person to be a false prophet. If you are wrong, the stigma is horrible and not easily undone.

I don't want to be a false prophet

I don't blame you. Here is the good news: There are more true prophets than false ones.

There tend to be two types of false prophets.

- The most obvious type: Many cults and religions claim to speak for their god. Members will prophesy in the name of another god. The information they give is false, or it may be accurate but demonically inspired.
- The less obvious type: They may claim to speak in the name of the one true God but can be recognized

as false by the fruit of their lives. They are prone to ungodly behaviors and attitudes; they will often take Scripture out of context for their own use and will sell their gifts to the person who gives the most. The prophet of God needs to be above being bought or sold for money or influence and needs to be no respecter of persons.

> Beware of false prophets, who come to you in sheep's clothing, but inwardly they are ravenous wolves. You will know them by their fruits. Do men gather grapes from thornbushes or figs from thistles? Even so, every good tree bears good fruit, but a bad tree bears bad fruit. A good tree cannot bear bad fruit, nor can a bad tree bear good fruit. . . . Therefore by their fruits you will know them.
>
> Matthew 7:15–18, 20

Let me describe for you some characteristics (fruit) of false prophets, so you can see how they operate, and we can contrast it against the fruit of a true prophet:

False prophets

- Presumptuous and proud in attitude (Deuteronomy 18:20; 1 Kings 13:18; 22:24; Jeremiah 23; Ezekiel 13).
- Bear bad fruit in their lives and ministries (Jeremiah 23:10–11, 14).

- Are consistently inaccurate in their prophecies (Deuteronomy 18:22; Jeremiah 23:11–32; Ezekiel 13:9–19).
- In cases when they do manage to prophesy accurately, their prophesying and teaching lead people away from worshiping and obeying only the Lord (Deuteronomy 13:2; 18:20).

True prophets

- Lead people to worship only the Lord.
- Bear good fruit in their lives and ministries (see the contrasts in Jeremiah 23:10–11, 14).
- Are consistently accurate in their prophecies (Deuteronomy 18:21–22).

This does not mean that true prophets never prophesied inaccurately. Scripture makes it clear that on occasion true prophets knowingly or unknowingly prophesied inaccurately and were not put to death or branded false prophets for such inaccuracies (2 Samuel 7:3; 1 Kings 22:15). Jeremiah seemed uncertain that he had heard the word of the Lord accurately until it was confirmed by corresponding events: "Then I *knew* that this was the word of the LORD" (Jeremiah 32:8, emphasis added). The implication was that, until that moment, Jeremiah was not certain that what he had heard was, indeed, a true word from the Lord.

It is possible for weakness or character defects to grow, which, if not corrected, will set you up to eventually become a false prophet or prophetess (1 Kings 13:18). People who initially followed false prophets such as Jim Jones have stated that these prophets initially started off as true ministers in the beginning. Eventually, Jim Jones went from being true to being completely deceitful. Just because people seem to display gifts doesn't mean they are true prophets of God. Character needs to match up with gifts.

A pastor I know went to hear Jim Jones when he was preaching in Los Angeles and shared how a person in the front jumped up and began to praise God. Jones commanded him to sit down, saying, "You're here to hear from me today. I taught you that, not God." The thought that it is possible to deteriorate from a true minister or prophet to a false one is very sobering. We need to keep the fear of the Lord upon our lives to keep us straight with God. Abide also in His Word, which is infallible and will aid in keeping you on the correct path.

Now, let's say someone gives a prophetic word, and even after many years, the prophesy is not fulfilled. There are two possible reasons for this.

1. The person being prophesied to does not meet the conditions the Lord gives in the prophecy or falls into sin (1 Samuel 10:1; 13:13–14).

2. The person prophesying did so out of the flesh or has only a partial understanding of what God was

saying—this affects what he or she is hearing from the Lord.

It's also important to note that human love can taint a word. I am careful about prophesying to people who are close to me because my own personal love for them and my emotions might get in the way of what God is really saying. Usually, I say, "I feel I am possibly hearing this prophetic word from the Lord for you, but I would like to have it confirmed by someone who doesn't know you as well (or doesn't have a vested interest in what happens)." Sometimes love can blind the prophet, causing him or her to give a good prophetic word when the Lord wants to give a word of correction. One needs to be especially careful when prophesying healing over someone with a terminal illness whom you know well. This does not mean that you are not standing in faith for their healing, however.

Waiting on God

Another area where people can get confused is in receiving a promise from the Lord and thinking God is going to fulfill that promise immediately. You may receive a prophetic word in which the Lord says, "*I will do this immediately,*" but the actual result may not occur for three years or more. However, God will begin to work behind the scenes now to set into motion the things that will bring about the fulfillment of the word.

I once heard a profound prophecy that said, "For I, the Lord, am a behind-the-scenes God. I am constantly working in ways you cannot see because if you knew what I was doing, you would get your hands into it and mess it up."

It doesn't necessarily have to take years for a word to come to pass. Sometimes it happens in a few days! The point is that we need to cling to the prophetic word and believe God has spoken, whether it takes one day or forty years to see the fruit. If it is truly a word from the Lord, it will come to pass.

God's Vocabulary

God can use allegories, typologies, and terminology to make His point. There are times when the Lord uses certain words that mean one thing to us, but quite another to Him. In his book *Prophets and Personal Prophecy*, Dr. Bill Hamon interprets some of the terms used by God in the Bible to indicate time:

- Immediately: This was used by Jesus to signal progressive growth and preparation. This usually can be interpreted as a period of one day to three years.
- Very soon: This typically means one to ten years.
- Now (or This day): This means one to forty years.
- I will: Without a time designation, this means God will act sometime in the person's life if that person remains obedient.

- Soon: This was the term Jesus used to describe the time of His soon return almost two thousand years ago (Revelation 22:12).[1]

These are guidelines. God is omnipotent; He exists beyond our limited understanding of time and space. So, while these interpretations are helpful and are drawn from how God used time references in Scripture, remember He can work when and how He chooses.

Knowing the Audience

The key to effective communication is to know your audience. The same is true in delivering prophetic words. When you are prophesying, it is important that you communicate in a way that will be understood by the person receiving the word. Ask yourself, "How would God speak to this person?" If you are giving a prophetic word to a child, then bellowing, "Thus sayeth the Lord!" in a booming voice would probably not be the right approach.

Before I deliver a prophecy to someone, these are some of the things I think about:

- How would the Lord speak to them?
- What voice and tone is the Lord using to speak to this person?
- Do I have any background knowledge on this person?

- Do I know their past experiences with the church?
- Am I being careful to use language that is as free of "Christianese" as possible?

Your aim as you prophesy or minister (in any manner, to anyone) should be to help that person receive the prophetic word from the Lord. You need to be careful that your style of ministry does not turn them off or keep him or her from receiving the prophetic word. Your job is both to receive the word from the Lord and to communicate it in the way that is most edifying to the person to whom you are ministering.

If you are ministering to children, please remember that the Lord loves them dearly. Adults are oftentimes rough as they minister to little ones, and this can hurt them or frighten them. My own daughter was literally pushed over by a minister who was praying for her when she was little. After that, she had a difficult time receiving prayer from anyone she did not know. Children consider the size of adults intimidating and do not like to be treated in a harsh or rough way by them.

Here are a few keys for ministering to children:

- First, ask them whether they want you to pray for them. Many times, adults drag children to the front of a church to be prayed for and years later the children are either hurt or resentful. No adult likes to be forced against his or her will to receive prayer, and neither do children. Teenagers especially resent this.

- Talk to them for a moment on a personal level. Ask them their names. If you perceive that they might be afraid or nervous, ask whether they feel comfortable having you pray for them. I sometimes tell them that I understand if they are nervous and that I once felt that way too, but that the Lord wants to bless them.

- Watch your tone of voice. You might want to stoop down to their level if they are very small. Don't use a religious tone of voice. Keep it gentle. Some Christians have an affected form of speech and deliver their words in a way that seems to be an attempt to make the message clear, but their delivery actually takes away from effectiveness. I would suggest you consider dropping any affectations and speak normally.

APPLICATION

Have you ever received a prophetic word, and it either didn't happen the way you thought, or it hasn't come to pass yet? What assumptions did you make about the person giving that word? Sometimes, if God's timing and our assumed timeline are not the same, we jump to conclusions about the validity of the word (and the validity of the one giving it).

I would like you to write the word in question on a piece of paper or play it if you have it recorded. Take note of any time-related words.

Remember, words like "immediately" or "soon" often do not mean "tomorrow by breakfast." Once you've had a few minutes to review what you were given, I'd like you to pray over this word. Ask the Holy Spirit to show you if there is any ungodly delay over this word, or any sin in your life that is hindering the word coming to pass. Ask that the Lord remove confusion or deception and repent of anything He brings to light. If this word is truly from the heart of God, ask for Him to give you peace and patience to wait on its fulfillment.

If you've made accusations against the prophetic person (in your heart or out loud), repent of that before the Lord. Is it possible the person giving the word was a false prophet? Well, yes. There is always that possibility. However, God will deal with that; your focus is to get your heart in order before the Lord.

6

Prophetic Callings and Prophetic Intercession

What does prayer have to do with prophecy? Everything. Remember that prophecy can be defined as a spontaneous, divinely-given understanding or foreknowledge about a person or an event. There are many different types of prophets and prophecy, but for those operating in their prophetic gifting, they cultivate a rich prayer life. Throughout the Scriptures, prophets sought God through prayer and going where they knew He could be found. They spent time with God, asking Him for His perspective and seeking His face in prayer. How can we hope to hear the voice of God and His will and heart toward us when we don't take time to speak with Him? If you want to truly lean in and learn the voice of God, I encourage you to set some time aside regularly to seek Him in prayer. Even if you can only set aside ten minutes a day, do that consistently.

Types and Styles of Prophets

Prophets are diverse. Each one has a unique style, flavor, and calling. Let's lay out some general groupings modeled from biblical examples of the prophets. The people I am about to talk about may be prophetic people who, although not standing in the office of the prophet, move in the gift of prophecy and/or are prophetic intercessors.

How a prophetic word is received from the Lord, as well as the method used to deliver the message, are clues used to identify the type of prophetic gift in which you or someone else operates.

The seer: They literally or figuratively see things in the spirit. Certain prophetic people today receive their prophetic words mainly through pictures. Their prophecies will often be interpretations of pictures or inner visions they see. Seers are usually emotionally empathetic people, but a word of caution—Satan will try to give counterfeit visions to those who are seers. I believe it is wise to ask the Lord to close your vision to those things He does not want you to see. If there is any occult or New Age influence, that needs to be renounced and cut off so the prophetic vision will not be affected by demonic influence.

Governmental prophets: Daniel would be a great example of a prophet of government. His prophecies spoke of monumental changes in the world order. There are just such prophets today, and some are actually in governmental positions. I have found that prophets seem to be sent to various institutions of society, such as legal, educational, and governmental offices. Governmental prophets are often also prophets to nations. I, for one, am both.

Counseling prophets: Some prophetic people may never give many public prophecies, but they possess a prophetic gift of counsel. They have a rare ability to point out pitfalls, serious problems, and consequences of people's actions in a manner that releases an enormous measure of grace to the hearer. Counseling is one area in which prophets are usually gifted because they are able to give a word of knowledge or wisdom supernaturally about a given situation. Examples from the Bible would be Nathan (2 Samuel 7:3; 1 Kings 1:24) or Huldah (2 Kings 22:14–20).

Weeping prophets: Some prophets are used by God in the area of weeping in intercession for nations. This kind of weeping is different from that caused by personal emotions. You may not feel the least bit sad, but you find tears coursing down your face and a godly sorrow pouring out as you prophesy or pray for a person. Jeremiah was used by God to pray for his nation (Jeremiah 9:10; 13:17; 14:17; Lamentations 1:16; 2:18; 3:48).

Prophetic dreamers: Prophetic dreamers will often be awakened by the Lord to intercede when warning dreams are given. They are called by God to take the night watch and are given keys to pray about in their dreams. One prophet, Thomas Hall, received a dream that held a key that opened Dutch Sheets's understanding to what is now a whole prophetic movement called Appeal to Heaven. My husband, Mike, is a prophetic dreamer and has often been given warnings of things that Satan was planning that we were able to stop or minimize through intercessory prayer.

Singing prophets/psalmists: David was certainly a good example of a singing prophet or psalmist. The book of Psalms is a songbook that includes many prophecies. Another example is when the prophet Deborah sang a song with Barak after the victory over Sisera (Judges 5). Coupled with the anointing on the music, prophetic song is a beautiful, powerful expression of this gift. I encourage you, even if you do not consider yourself musically gifted, to lift up your voice in song before the Lord and see if He puts something on your heart to sing or play.

Prophets of prophetic administration, or Issachar prophets —what I call the Joseph anointing: The Josephs who have prophetic anointing are raised up and put into positions of authority to bring order and release of finances in economic systems. God gives them supernatural strategies as He gave Joseph for Egypt before the years of plenty and years of famine. Some people are gifted in the area of administration and are able to bring order to organizations within a short time period.

Our friend Chuck Pierce is one of the most accurate Issachar prophets we have known. We have known him to give precise dates, such as when we were moving back to Dallas from Colorado Springs, and he said we needed to move by an exact date. We were able to make the transition exactly in the time frame that he gave us. He says, "Timing is important, so we can set God's timing for the future." He also prophesied in St. Louis, a city right near Ferguson, Missouri, where the shooting of an African American youth by a white policeman sparked race riots. His word was that the area would be the dividing line for the nation. I believe this word was given as a prophetic warning and call for prayer.

Prophets to the nations: This would include those who have a call to minister in the nations of the world. Some will travel and prophesy in many nations, and their theme Scripture is often Psalm 2:8 or Isaiah 49:6. Others will be called to their own nations as prophets, and the words they receive will center around their nations.

Kris Vallotton of Bethel Church in Redding, California, received his call as a prophet to the nations some twenty-five years ago. At the time, he was a mechanic and did not seem a likely candidate for the prophetic work he is doing today alongside Bill Johnson. During his prayer time one day, he had a visitation from the Lord in which Jesus told him he would be a prophet to the nations and guide the hearts of kings, prime ministers, and presidents. The Lord then said, *"This is My plan for you, and history will tell if you believe*

Me." Kris was waiting to follow that call, but he kept declining messages from governmental leaders because he didn't seem to have any prophetic words for them.

One day, I was in Redding, and he asked if I would meet with him and pray over him. He told me that he was turning down meetings with governmental leaders because he didn't believe he was receiving anything. I told him I also don't get words for leaders until I go in and sit down with them. Kris decided to follow that pattern and met with the next governmental leader who invited him. He not only received a prophecy, but it was an extremely detailed word that has changed lives and, no doubt, nations.

Prophetic orators and teachers: These people are gifted to communicate God's prophetic messages. They are like silver-tongued Isaiah and will be moved to give lengthy prophetic messages. Not all of the messages will be spontaneous—some may come in the form of prophetic teaching. As a result of studying God's Word, the Lord will give revelatory messages that will be a trumpeting of what the Holy Spirit is saying to the Church.

Prophets to the local church: I personally believe that God calls one or more prophets to each local church. They may not be recognized as such, and their prophesying may take the form of prophetic intercession, but they will hear accurately from the Lord. In his book *Prayer Shield*, C. Peter Wagner points out that some intercessors are assigned by God to pray and accurately share with the pastor the information they hear from the Lord. Although these people may not be seated in the office of a prophet, they certainly are prophetic in their gifting.

The Deborah anointing: God has called some prophetesses to be Deborahs. They have spirits of wisdom and counsel and are often spiritual warriors. They have strong gifts of leadership, and many times the Lord will couple them with Baraks as seen in Judges 4.

What Does Prophetic Intercession Look Like?

My first call is actually that of a prophetic intercessor; this is a part of my life with the Lord that I know and love very dearly. Many times, I have awakened my husband, Mike, in the night to pray over a pending terrorist attack. One night, I said, "Mike, someone is going to try and blow up an airplane coming to the United States! We need to pray!" He looked at me with groggy eyes and replied "Okay, you pray, and I will agree!" Later on, a terrorist was caught, now remembered as the Shoe Bomber. I am sure other prophetic intercessors were alerted as well, but the key here is that when I heard the prayer request from God, I went straight to intercession.

Prophetic intercession is the ability to receive an immediate prayer request from God and pray about it in a divinely-anointed utterance. Biblical examples can be found throughout Scripture (Genesis 18:20–23; Exodus 32:7–14; Daniel 9:1–4, 20–22; Luke 2:36–38; 22:31–32; John 17; Acts 9:10–17;

22:17–21). Many times, such prayer requests come in the form of prophetic words. The people praying may not realize this at the time and only later find out it was God speaking to them to pray prophetically.

Prophetic intercession is important not only for people, but for nations as well. Many people are obeying God by praying for revival, but when revival finally comes, they stop praying for the protection of the harvest God has given. Revival does not always run like clockwork without problems; it requires prophetic intercessors, mentors, and strong, godly community for the young Christians. Norman Grubb pinpointed a lack of intercession as being a problem during the 1904 Welsh Revival.

> But the real problem arose as the Revival proceeded and thousands were added to the churches. As enthusiasm abated, there were bound to be many who had depended more on feelings, and not yet learned to have their faith solidly based on the word of God. The devil took advantage of this, some became cold and indifferent, and the spiritual conflict began. Those like Rees Howells, young in the Spirit though they were, but at least a bit more advanced than the converts in the revival, were needed to be intercessors and teachers, to take the burden of the newborn babes, and pray and lead them. But these young intercessors soon began to find how mighty is the enemy of souls, and that a conflict, not against flesh and blood, but against the rulers of the darkness of this world, cannot be fought with carnal weapons. "Many blamed

the young converts for backsliding," he said, "but we blamed ourselves, because we were not in a position to pray them through to victory. Oh, the tragedy, to be helpless in front of the enemy, when he was sifting young converts like wheat!"[1]

"All Prophets Are Intercessors"

In the beginning of my development as a prophetic voice, the how-tos were still very much a mystery to me. I knew the Lord seemed to be using me to pray prophetically, but I didn't have much grasp of the scriptural basis for prophetic intercession or personal prophecy. One day I was riding in a car with my friend Margaret Moberly, who taught me quite a bit about prophesying. She said, "Cindy, not all intercessors are prophetic, but all prophets are intercessors!" She quoted Jeremiah 27:18, which gives direct instruction to prophets to make intercession to the Lord of hosts. This was like a lightbulb moment for me. At that time, I didn't think I was a prophet, but I knew I could intercede prophetically.

As the years have gone by, I have increasingly understood how interwoven intercession is with prophecy. Although many prophets do not consider themselves intercessors, they spend long hours in intimacy with the Father, listening and praying. Look at the life of Abraham. God spoke to Abraham and told him beforehand that He was going to destroy Sodom and Gomorrah. Abraham immediately began prophetic intercession for the righteous in the city.

Interestingly enough, one of the pictures given to us through the interceding of Abraham in Genesis 18 conveys the meaning of the prophet as a legal defender in the court of heaven, presenting a case before God as Judge. At times when we pray, we stand in the gap as a prosecutor or legal defender, God having spoken a prophetic word to us concerning another person or a nation. We pray according to the revelation given to us in the prophecy.

Training for the Prophetic

Intercession is a training ground for the prophetic gifts. I personally believe that almost all prophetic intercessors have the ability to prophesy on a regular basis or to become prophets. As intercessors begin to regularly experience answers to their prayers from supernatural knowledge given to them by God, many step forward to share with a trusted friend or mentor what they are sensing.

At times, this kind of praying involves a progressive revelation of God's will. One day when I was interceding, I kept hearing a man's name. I heard no other words, but I felt great alarm for this man. I prayed, "Father, protect him, encourage him. Don't let him do anything he shouldn't do." The next day, I received a prayer request for a well-known traveling evangelist who was struggling with great discouragement. He had the same name I had been hearing, and I could then pray with greater knowledge. I strongly sense the Lord may have averted a suicide attempt—the situation was dire at that moment. When we receive something like this from the Lord, and we discern it is truly Him, it is important that we jump straight into prayer. Timing may be of the essence.

Prophetic intercession often catches unaware those who are praying. At times, a person may begin praying a simple prayer of petition when, all of a sudden, the tonality of their voice will change. A ring of authority comes. It is as though the intercessor has shifted gears in the Spirit as the power of the Holy Spirit energizes the prayer.

One important aspect of prayer as a training ground for the prophetic is that it confirms we are actually hearing from God. Very few people who move in personal prophecy (standing in front of a person and giving a prophetic word on a regular basis) started out at this point. Most started as I did, by praying for people and having them exclaim, "How did you know to pray that way?"

Prophetic intercessors often receive rather strenuous training from the Lord. He requires things—to temper them—that may seem more than a little unusual to others. Some people might wonder at the strictness and, at times, the severity of the training prophets undergo. Although God may vary the severity of His preparation depending on the person, His training is stretching and demanding on those being trained, no matter what their calling. I have found, however, that the greater the calling and responsibilities God plans to give a prophet, the more exacting and, at times, lengthy the preparation for the call. Romans 11:22 says, "Therefore consider the goodness and severity of God." We know it is a biblical principal that unto whom much is given, much is required (Luke 12:48).

Above all, we need time in His presence, in prayer, to build our intimacy with the Lord. For me to persevere in the walk God has for me, it is necessary for me to spend at least one, but usually two to three hours a day in His presence. As you are going through whatever testing the Lord has for you, I encourage you to review at the end of each day and ask the Holy Spirit to show you where there are roots of sin or moments where you acted out of the flesh. Keep a short account with the Lord, learn from failures, and persevere in the testing by staying close to Him and in His Word.

Hear and Obey

As a person is trained to prophesy, the Lord will often work intensively in the area of obedience. There are special strategic "windows of time" not only to pray, but also to obey by doing a physical act that might be called an intercessory act or a prophetic act. At times, such acts may seem a bit unusual, but they can be powerful in breaking down strongholds. And still, at other times, we may be more traditional in what we consider intercession. The typical view of intercession would be to gather in a prayer room or to kneel in our prayer closets (places where we can go regularly for quiet time with God).

In Joshua 6, prophetic instructions were given regarding how to take Jericho through an intercessory act. The same God who told the Israelites to march around Jericho also told them to stand firm in the face of invading enemies, so they sent worshipers before the army and prevailed (2 Chronicles 20:15–22). The prophet Jeremiah was instructed to hide his girdle among some rocks where water would shrink it as a sign from the Lord in Jeremiah 13. Sometimes, the instructions just seem strange at first.

In the late 1970s, the Lord began to train me in obedience. One winter day as I prayed, the Lord seemed to say that I should go to a certain lighting shop to look for a fixture for my hallway. I hadn't planned to go at that time, but it seemed crucial that I go now. I gathered up my three-year-old daughter and my infant son and drove to the store. As I approached the store, I could see they were having a closeout sale. I thought, "How nice, the Lord is trying to save me some money." If I had known what God really wanted me to do when I got into the store, I would probably have turned and went home.

I found the fixture I needed, and as I was purchasing it, I asked the Jewish man who owned the store, "Why are you selling out?" He looked very sad and said in a quiet voice, "I am very ill and the doctors don't know what is wrong with me. They have given me handfuls of pills to take, but I'm getting worse. I simply can't run my store anymore."

All of a sudden, I had one of those strange feelings. I grabbed my children and tried to get out of the store before

. . . that still, small voice interrupted me halfway through the store. "*Cindy, I want you to go lay hands on him, and I'm going to heal him.*"

"Heal him, Lord? You mean You want me to walk up to him and pray for him in the name of Jesus? Lord, he's Jewish. Won't he be offended or turn me down flat?" Again, the voice of the Lord spoke, "*Cindy, I want you to . . .*" I admit, I interrupted that voice. "Okay, okay! I'll do it." Not feeling the least bit brave or anointed, I shepherded the kids back to the man. He looked up in surprise. "Have you forgotten something?"

My heart was thundering in my chest as I murmured, "Sir, may I pray for you?" I didn't tell him I was going to pray in the name of Jesus, because I was too chicken. I quickly laid my hands on him and blurted out, "In the name of Jesus, be healed!" You know, he didn't hit me or anything! A few weeks later, I went back to the store owner, gathered up my courage, and said, "Excuse me, but I'm the lady who prayed for you a couple of weeks ago, and I've been wondering how you are feeling." I was shocked when he grabbed me by the shoulders with big tears in his eyes. "You! You're the one who prayed? I went back to my doctor, and they can't find the problem anymore. I seem to be perfectly healthy now!"

First Thessalonians 5:21 says, "Test all things; hold fast what is good." Practice obeying that still, small voice. As you go, you will start to understand when the impressions are from the Lord and when they are simply your own flesh and mind.

<hr />

APPLICATION

First, go back to the types of prophets at the beginning of this chapter. Read through those descriptions again. Do any of them resonate with your own journey? Are there moments in your life when you have been awakened from dreams? Are you a weeping prophet, a seer, or do you perhaps have a Deborah anointing? If you aren't sure, don't worry. Go before the Lord and ask Him to clarify where your gifting lies.

The second part of this application is to spend some dedicated time in God's presence a few times throughout the week. Maybe set aside the time you would use in the evening to scroll online, or to watch your favorite show. Take that time and go to your prayer closet. Sit with the Lord, be still, and ask Him, "What do You want to speak to me today?" If you feel yourself getting distracted, ask the Lord to remove any distractions, and don't be discouraged. Sit, wait, listen. If He shares something, I encourage you to write it down so you can pray into it further.

— 7 —

Dreams and Visions

You may have very strong opinions on this topic because of your church background. Some churches teach that the miracles and ways God spoke to His people in the Bible are only in the past. They don't believe that God still speaks to His people through dreams and visions. There is zero biblical evidence to support that theory; in fact, the Bible is full of stories about dreams and visions in both the Old and New Testaments. Although it may seem strange to those reading this book who are of a Western worldview, God still speaks to His people through visions or dreams today.

In Job 33:14–16 we read, "For God may speak in one way, or in another, yet man does not perceive it. In a dream, in a vision of the night, when deep sleep falls upon men, while slumbering on their beds, then He opens the ears of men, and seals their instruction."

The Bible shows that the Holy Spirit often spoke through dreams that caused critical changes in people's lives and the history of nations. Dreams played a particularly significant role in the birth of the Messiah. Without the dream where an angel of God spoke to Joseph, Mary may have been stoned or at least put away (Matthew 1:20–23). In fact, in the first two chapters of Matthew's gospel, we see no fewer than five dreams. God spoke to the Pharaoh of Egypt to alert him that seven years of plenty and seven years of famine would impact his nation. He then sent Joseph to interpret that dream, and the nation of Egypt was prepared for the coming times of hardship.

It is not uncommon for God to speak to His people in dreams. Unfortunately, many people ignore most of their dreams, or they wait so long to write them down that they forget them. Those who have a prophetic gifting will remember their dreams more often; God says in His Word that this is one way He speaks to His prophets. For some prophets, dreams are one of the main ways God speaks to them (Joel 2:28; Genesis 28:12; 31:10–11; 37:5–9; Matthew 1:20; 2:13, 19).

My entire family has prophetic dreams from time to time. In my book *Possessing the Gates of the Enemy*, I tell the story about the warning dreams my husband, Mike, had for our family. One of the most frequent warning dreams is of tornadoes coming at our house or at other people. We know these are not fate, but rather the Lord wanting us to pray and avert what is coming.

Interpreting Dreams

Here are some specific things to do if you have a vivid prophetic dream:

- Ask whether it is from the Lord or not. Satan can send tormenting or deceptive dreams (Ecclesiastes 5:3, 7). For instance, if a married woman dreams she is married to another man, this would not be a prophetic dream from God guiding her to divorce her husband and marry someone else; that would be a lying dream.

- Write it down so you will remember the details. It's a great idea to keep a notepad and pen by your bed just for this reason.

- Pray for the interpretation. If you are not able to interpret it yourself, ask the Lord to send someone to you who can. I have found that the Lord will often let me know when a circumstance fits a dream I've had. The dream will come to my remembrance, and it will be like the pieces of a puzzle fitting together.

- If the dream remains a mystery to you and no one else is able to interpret it at that time, don't throw it away. If you sense it is from the Lord, keep it somewhere for a later time. Dreams can be like time-release capsules and can come to pass years later.

- Be careful with whom you share the dream. Like Joseph sharing his dreams with his brothers (whose hearts were definitely not ready), you may tell your dream too soon, and it may seem outlandish or prideful—especially if it seems rather grandiose. Years ago, I had dreams of speaking to packed stadiums, praying for the sick, and seeing many dramatic healings. I waited to share those dreams with anyone, and then, only just a few people. Today, the night visions I saw long ago are coming to pass.

- If the dream seems to indicate a change in your life's direction, seek guidance from those in spiritual authority to confirm what you believe God is saying to you.

- The dream may be for someone else. Ask the Lord if and/or when you should share it with the person. It may be something you need to pray about yourself, thus allowing the Lord to avert the situation without worrying the other person. One of my prayer partners was greatly disturbed when she had a dream that I had died in a shipwreck. She woke up and prayed for me and also shared it with my sister, who prayed about it. Later, my sister told me about the dream. I understood immediately what it was about. In the past, I have preached a sermon on being shipwrecked in faith. At the time, I was totally overwhelmed with many responsibilities, and the pressure was so heavy that I felt as though I was drowning. Perhaps these two intercessors averted some physical disaster that might have been brought on by such stress.

- If the Lord is giving a warning, pray about it. Seek wisdom from someone you trust. It may be that you need to share it with your prayer group. At times, God gives a warning dream so you can "sound the alarm" for disaster or judgment to be averted.

Visions

What is the difference between a dream and a vision? In their teachings, John and Paula Sandford called visions "the picture language of God."[1] They go on to state that the important difference between dreams and visions is that when we receive a vision, we are awake. Visions are much more subject to our control, and they come in many degrees. Sometimes, the Holy Spirit flashes pictures across the inner screens of our minds with or without interruption of conscious thoughts. It is possible to receive a vision and to stop it in the middle portion. I believe we can resist what we are seeing, shake it off, scoff at it, and likely abort what God is trying to show in that moment.

Some think visions are less "in the Spirit" because they happen less dramatically than trances (which we will cover in a moment). This is not so. God simply chooses how He will communicate to us according to His wisdom. Such visions are not less valuable, forceful, imperative, or truthful.

My first full-blown vision happened when Mike and I were flying to Africa in 1979. He had been laid off from his job with Trans-World Airlines and we had one trip pass left. We were discussing the future, and I was saying, "Mike, what would you like to do for a job anyway?" About that time, the in-flight movie came on. When I looked at the screen, it looked like another screen had been rolled over the movie screen, and I began to have a vision. This vision was of an airplane. It was sitting in a hangar and seemed to belong to Mike. I saw him kneeling down, praying with two other men in a lovely office, and one of the men had beautiful silver hair. When the vision ended, I described the airplane to Mike. He said, "Honey, as far as I know, no plane like that exists." Years later, he came to me with a magazine about flying and showed me a picture of an airplane. "Is this the plane you saw in your vision?" he asked. Astounded, I looked at the picture of the plane I had seen in the vision years before. It was one and the same—the Falcon 900, a private business jet that has transatlantic capabilities.

Visions are often progressive. God told Abram to leave and go to the land of promise (Genesis 12:1–2). Later, God told Abram He would make his descendants like the dust of the earth (Genesis 13:16). God often gives us just what we need for the present season of our lives and adds to it when there is a change, shift, or addition to what He said previously.

There are three categories of visions:

- Open vision: The vision seems as real as anything else going on around you. You feel and see as if you are really in the vision. Angelic visitations fall into this category. You are able to "see" into the dimension in which the angels exist. Gideon's visitation with the angel of the Lord would be an example of this (Judges 6:11). Cornelius "saw clearly in a vision an angel of God coming in" (Acts 10:3). It is interesting that Cornelius was a God-fearing man, but he was not a Christian. The use of visions and dreams given to unbelievers has been a powerful factor in many of them coming to Christ.

- Inner vision: This may not feel as strong as an open vision. You may picture something in your mind. Once I could not find my passport, and after searching fruitlessly for days, I decided to ask the Lord where it was. My husband said, "Cindy, calm down and just get quiet before the Lord so you can hear Him." I did this, and I immediately had a flash of insight: I knew to look in our tall dresser behind the top left drawer. In a matter of seconds, I opened the drawer and had the passport in my hand. If this had been an open vision, I would have felt like I actually saw the drawer, and it would have seemed as real as anything else around me. This was an inner vision, because I had an inner knowing of exactly where it was, like a picture in my mind.

- Trances: Acts 10 shows examples of a person having a vision and another falling into a trance. This is the portion of Scripture where Peter was on the roof and the sheet filled with animals was lowered to him. Now, a trance is a much deeper expression than a vision. It seems that when God causes someone to fall into a trance, it supersedes all else. In fact, the Greek word for "trance" used in Acts 10:10 means a displacement of the mind, or "ecstasy." Saul's meeting with God on the road to Damascus could be considered a deeper trancelike experience (Acts 9:3–6), although Paul himself refers to it as a vision in Acts 26:19.

I have a story of a trance encounter with the Lord that comes from my own family. My sister Lucy married a fine young man named Mark. The only problem was that Mark wasn't a Christian, and Lucy, although she was raised in a Christian home, had wandered far away from Christ. I prayed for almost six years, and finally she gave her heart back to God. She then joined me in praying for her husband's salvation.

Mark came from a Presbyterian background. In college, he was swayed by humanism, and at the same time, life's disappointments caused him to doubt if God was real. He never really came to the point of denying the existence of God, but was more like the perfect agnostic. For six years, I prayed and fasted and interceded for Mark's salvation. During those years, Mike and I would speak with Mark from time to time, but most often it did not end well. This wasn't because of anything Mark did; we were battling against spiritual forces of darkness that were very afraid of Mark coming to Christ.

Some people need a supernatural visitation from God completely outside of what can be grasped from a natural understanding. With his background in science and reliance on reason, Mark was one of those people. One night, a voice awakened Mark. It was the same voice Saul heard on the road to Damascus. "*Mark, I am the one you are resisting. I am God!*" Mark's room lit up with a bright light, and at that moment he knew Jesus was the only way to heaven and that He was God. My sister slept through the entire encounter, and Mark gave his life to Christ.

Throughout Church history, we hear of true believers falling into a trance. However, let me give the caution that deception is possible. In some counterfeit religions, people meditate to go into a trance state. This is not the same thing as God visiting you with a trance. You cannot force your way into a trance. God gives a trance as a result of an outpouring of His Spirit, or it may come upon you sovereignly as it did when Peter fell into a trance on the roof.

Getting Practical: Prophetic Gifts in Practice

Now that we have identified these different ways God speaks to His children, let's get practical. Maybe you have prophesied, or you have had a few friends say to you, "I think you have the gift of prophecy." You might! One of your prayers over someone else may become a prophecy for them, which is a safe way to begin putting this into practice. Here are a few steps to stepping out and exercising these prophetic muscles.

The first step is that you hear from God. It is my personal belief that everyone in the Body of Christ does occasionally experience—in some way—supernatural knowledge of things to come without the person being aware of it. Maybe it's just a feeling, and then later the things you felt would actually come to pass. God gives parents who are praying for their children many of these impressions so they will know how to intercede for them when they are in a mess, in danger, or upset. They may not know what to do with what they are hearing from God or recognize that it is the Lord wanting them to pray prophetically to avert the danger. I encourage you to spend ample time with the Lord as we discussed. If you are spending personal time in the Word and in the presence of God, you will likely be able to hear His voice with growing clarity.

The second step is knowing if this is the time to release the prophetic word. We covered that in Chapter 5, so please go back and review. Timing does matter!

The third step is to determine if what you are receiving is a prophetic word or an impression. An impression is vague, usually just sensing something from the Lord. I believe an impression is a feeling that God is communicating to you, but it isn't as crystal-clear as when the Lord is speaking a direct word of prophecy. When you are preparing to give a prophetic word about a person or a group of people, while you are alone (not in front of the people themselves), it will probably come as words that form inside your spirit. The Lord will speak the same things again and again. At times, you may feel as though a balloon has been blown up within your inner person. If it is not the right time to give the word, submit it back to the Lord for His direction and timing, and wait for the appropriate time to share it.

Unless you are a recognized prophet or prophetess in the Body of Christ, I would be cautious about giving a prophecy in the first person ("I, your God, say . . ." or "This is what God is saying"). Even those who are set into the office of prophet should be careful about using the first person and should do so with the fear of the Lord upon their lives.

If you are really not sure if what you are hearing is a clear word, you can say, "This isn't strong and clear enough for me to call it a prophetic word, but I do have the impression that your current situation will clear up in two years' time."

At times, God will veil from the prophet what He is saying to the person receiving the prophecy. The word may be between God and the person receiving it. On other occasions, God will give the word in a riddle or symbol that will require prayer and seeking Him for the answer (Amos 7:8; 8:2; Acts 10:11–12).

If you are sure it is the Lord speaking, I would say so. Remember that when giving a prophetic word, humility is very important; if you aren't sure, you can be honest. But if it is so strongly the word of God, you can give it as such. If you are going to give a prophetic word, and you believe it is from God, do not give it in veiled terms. Shoot straight, be able to stand behind it, and ask the Lord what He means.

The fourth step is to ascertain if you are on target with the person you are giving the word to. There will definitely be times when you need to move out in faith (as I had to with the Jewish man in his shop). Trust that God will honor that if it is from Him, and will equip you with what you need. However, another way to find out whether you should share with that person what you believe you are hearing from God is through the interview method.

The interview method is simply probing the person through questions to get some kind of feedback. For instance, if you think you have a prophetic word about a person's daughter, you might ask, "Do you have a daughter?" If the answer is yes, and what you think you've heard from the Lord is that the daughter is sick, you could proceed with,

"Does she have any physical problems?" If the answer is no, don't give up yet. The sickness may be emotional or relational. The word may need to be fine-tuned; you may have heard a partial word.

Ask a few more questions along the lines of what I suggested regarding other kinds of possible problems or sicknesses. Usually something surfaces about which you can pray, and the impression you received from the Lord will become clearer to you. Ask the person if it is all right to pray with him or her for the daughter. I always like to get people's permission to pray for them; it opens their hearts to the Lord and His power. If they are uncomfortable about praying at that time (which sometimes happens), tell them you will pray for the daughter later by yourself. Leave them with the knowledge that God cares deeply for them and their daughter.

APPLICATION

What were you taught in church about prophetic dreams and visions? Take a moment and think back on a time when you had a vivid dream (or a series of dreams, or a dream that repeated). So many people say, "I don't remember my dreams!" However, we all have had a dream that was either very strong or kept coming back. Now, did anything come of that dream? Did you alter something in your life, or did the things you dreamed happen?

I would encourage you to keep a journal and pen (or your phone with its recording function) next to your bed. If you have a vivid dream or God wakes you up with a word, jot it down with as much detail as you can remember. Pray into that word.

I also encourage you to keep a record of times when you have an inner picture (or a full open vision, though those are not as common). Write where you were, what you felt, and what it later revealed to you. By keeping track of both the dreams and inner knowings you receive, I think you will be surprised at how often God is speaking to you.

8

I Need Help! Mentoring the Prophetic Gift

Years ago, as a young person whose prophetic gift was beginning to emerge, I had a propensity to stick my foot in my mouth. It seemed as though I was in trouble more than I was out of it. I couldn't understand what I was doing wrong. I was particularly struggling with bad timing when I shared prophecies, harshness in my delivery, and pride: I was "*the* one hearing from God." During one particular prayer meeting, I was in rare form. A friend's daughter was visiting, and I discerned the young lady had a drug problem. Without finding out anything about her situation, I pointed my finger at her and said with a loud voice full of drama, "You have a demon of drugs!" Ouch! The girl completely freaked out. Her mother had worked with her for weeks to try to get her to attend church, and I blew the whole thing. I feel rather embarrassed now just thinking about my behavior.

Needless to say, the Lord started putting some pressure on me to change, but I just didn't fully understand what He was trying to tell me. Little did I know that God was mercifully trying to get me to a place where I could cry for help. One day, I lay flat on my face in my laundry room (of all the dignified places) and pleaded with God to send someone to teach and train me. I didn't even know what that looked like, but I desperately needed mentoring. I'm sure the Lord sighed from heaven, "*Finally, she realizes she can't do it all by herself.*"

Through the years, the Lord answered my prayer by sending many people along my path to help me. I've often joked, "I guess I was such a hard case that just one wasn't enough." Many leaders have influenced my life at various stages and for different seasons.

What Is a Mentorship and Why Does It Matter?

As I have traveled around the world and observed many cities, I have come to the opinion that many generations are fatherless and motherless, and that includes people within the Church. In other words, these generations are basically dysfunctional from a lack of spiritual parenting. More mature Christians may wonder why the next generation of believers is acting a certain way, but the truth is there is a serious lack of mentors in the faith. Most of the patterning we see in these young people comes from them observing very visible but distant leaders, without receiving much—if any—accountability. It is very sad to listen to pastors in their thirties and forties say, "Where are the fathers and mothers in the Gospel for my city? Isn't there anyone from whom I can learn?"

Some young, promising leaders have suffered abandonment from the very leaders who could have been their mentors. Some have been rejected by their leadership just as their spiritual gifts were maturing, or they were judged harshly by the person who was supposed to be a father or mother in the faith. Oftentimes, that rejection was because the leader suffered from jealousy and a fear of losing their position as they observed their mentee growing and perhaps moving beyond them. In such cases, the young ones often turned and ran; many new churches have been started from such beginnings. I believe it is safe to say in a prophetic way that God is looking for fathers and mothers in the faith, people who are willing to pay the price to learn how to mentor and parent the new generation of powerful leaders God is raising up across the world.

Robert Clinton of Fuller Theological Seminary gives this definition of mentoring:

> Mentoring refers to the process where a person with a serving, giving, encouraging attitude, the mentor, sees leadership

potential in a still-to-be developed person, the protégé, and is able to promote or otherwise significantly influence the protégé along in the realization of potential. . . . A mentor is someone who helps a protégé in some very practical ways: by giving timely advice that encourages the protégé; by risking his or her own reputation in backing the protégé; by bridging between the protégé and needed resources; by modeling and setting expectations that challenge the protégé; by giving tracts, letters, books or other literary information that opens perspectives for the protégé; by giving financially, sometimes sacrificially, to further the protégé's ministry; by co-ministering in order to increase the credibility, status, and prestige of the protégé; and by having the freedom to allow and even promote the protégé beyond the mentor's own level of leadership.[1]

That is a very tall order. I am not surprised that many older believers don't prioritize mentorship, but the truth is they need to. We are speaking about the future leaders of the Body of Christ. Mentorship is absolutely necessary for God's Church to flourish in the generations to come.

Receiving Mentoring

If the Lord brings you a mentor, you can take certain steps to make the most of the relationship. It does not matter if you are thirteen or seventy-three. If you are receiving mentorship, there are certain things you want to keep in mind:

- Have a teachable spirit: No one wants to work with a know-it-all who has an argumentative spirit. Some people always have their defensive shields up and carry a chip on their shoulder. This is a shame because it makes them difficult to mentor. When a mentor is giving us advice or correction, a good rule is not to close up immediately and try to justify ourselves. Instead, take it to the Lord. I've found that those who won't listen to the wounds of a friend (Proverbs 27:6) will have extremely painful experiences with enemies who are trying to correct them.

- Don't be demanding: Often, people only want to take from leaders without thinking of them as individuals. As someone who mentors many young people in prophetic ministry, my heart is warmed by those who want to give without demanding anything in return. I don't mind investing quite a bit of time to see that they receive all they need in the way of mentoring. Conversely, some people are petulant and follow leaders around, demanding time from them and then becoming angry when the leaders can't comply. Pushy people are a thorn in the side of busy leaders, and I rarely have anything to do with them unless the Lord really speaks to me to help them.

- Be self-initiating: Those who grow fastest are those who do not sit around and wait to be spoon-fed by their teachers, but instead study and glean from every godly source they can. Some of my students have positively delighted me by bringing a nugget of gold they have dug out of the Word that I had not seen myself. I sincerely desire my students to grow beyond where I have been, and it is my opinion that each succeeding generation should surpass the one that came before it.

- Submit to a local church: I have seen some young leaders refuse to submit to a pastor because they claim the pastor "just doesn't understand my gift." This is haughtiness in the highest form. If you pray, God will send you to the right church and to the right pastor. However, it may not be the church you like in the form you would personally enjoy. In certain stages of development, the Lord might have you submit to a pastor who doesn't have a handle on everything you do prophetically, but he has deep wells of wisdom and common sense you need to absorb.

Becoming a Mentor

Mentoring is a large responsibility, but it is so rewarding. Watching the next generation of leaders grow in their walk with God, hearing their stories as they experience Him, and letting God mold you as you mold others is so rich. So, let's take a look at some commonly asked questions and expectations about what this entails:

Who is qualified?

Maybe you are reading this and feeling that familiar prick in your heart. God may be calling you into the role of mentorship. On the other hand, if your life is really not in a stable or healthy place, or if you are struggling with family emergencies, illnesses, etc., then you may not be called at this time. I recommend going before the Lord and asking Him (1) if He desires you to be in a mentorship role, and (2) who He would like you to mentor.

When God calls you to be a leader, whether you like it or not, you will become a mentor to those who listen to you, are affiliated with you, and watch you. This may be uncomfortable to some, but it simply goes with the territory; it is part of the responsibility of a leader. Among those in leadership, some will have a special calling to mentor and raise up young leaders behind them.

What does it entail?

Mentorship is not just a title or a position; it is first and foremost a relationship. It is a real art, but I believe that one of the hallmarks of a good leader is the ability to replicate themselves in the anointing God has given them.

Mentoring does not consider physical age as a qualifying factor regarding whom to train. It is common for people who are ten or twenty years older than I am to consider me their teacher. I even receive Mother's Day cards from some of them, thanking me for being there for them when they needed counsel or advice.

Some mentoring relationships will last only a season, and some will last for a lifetime. The Lord brought Ruth and Naomi together for a lifelong relationship. Esther and Mordecai were relatives whom God called for His purposes for a nation. Look at Paul and Timothy in the New Testament! However long the relationship lasts, please be aware that mentees can fall into traps laid by the enemy, and it is important that you know what they are. Here are some common pitfalls your mentee may face:

Presumption: One of the greatest problems a young prophet can have is an attitude of presumption. The person hears something from God and immediately moves on it. Presumption comes from presuming we know what to do without checking it with other leaders. Prophets who are not properly tempered have one speed: fast-forward. This can cause some tension, as pastors often want to move at a slower pace in order for everyone in their congregation to enter the new things of God, and prophets can be so busy trying to accomplish a goal that they rush ahead. I believe that by working together, pastor and prophet can get the mind of the Lord on His timing; a prophetic voice must be willing to submit to the pastor as the authority. A good mentor will work with an emerging prophetic voice in the area of personal pacing—working with the pastoral leadership—and understand when to move out into ministry under God's commissioning, in His timing.

134

Insecurity: Many insecurities originate out of a fear of man (or woman). The Bible says that the "fear of man brings a snare" (Proverbs 29:25). The word for "snare" in the Hebrew means "bait or a lure in a fowler's net." Fearing humans goes along with pleasing humans. Not all prophetic words are pleasant, but when we are in the right timing and have the right heart, attitude, and wording, grace is the spoonful of sugar that helps the medicine go down. Caring too much about every little thing someone says to you, or assuming what they may think, is crippling. You are never free to just be yourself. The other extreme is not caring at all what others think, charging ahead, and consequently hurting people. A good mentor will help find the balance between these two extremes.

Inferiority: Inferiority is actually akin to insecurity. People who feel inferior will often mask it with "hostile humor." They will cut others down in order to build themselves up, but they will do it in a joking or sarcastic manner. This is also a sign of a critical spirit. Another indicator is excessive boasting, and I have seen this in both mentors and mentees. Let me clarify: It is not boasting to share testimonies from the places where we have ministered and what the Lord has done. Some people, however, always have to top everyone else's story. Frankly, I find this rather obnoxious. Experienced prophets and mentors must work to not be blasé about the testimonies of their younger leaders. The same way you would not overshadow the artwork of a child because you are more mature and can create something better, you must be careful to not try to "top" the stories your mentees bring you of God's power at work.

Rejection: Rejection is a real crippler when it comes to being accurate in the prophetic realm. Old wounds leak out and color what we say, often because we are trying to avoid being rejected again. Many leaders carry battle scars from past times when they gave prophetic words and they weren't received or they were misunderstood. If you have experienced this in your own ministry, you must be careful that bitter roots do not spring up in you and defile the student (Hebrews 12:15). This is extremely important, because young leaders will often hang on to your words as if they are gospel. Whether you like it or not, if you have any biases or bitterness, those whom you are teaching will pick up on them.

Pride: Your mentee may be tempted to indulge in pride, especially as they grow and they have incredible testimonies. As the mentor, help your mentees stay grounded and humble before the Lord. Another place pride springs up is when we are sharing teachings. There is no copyright on God's revelation. Give credit where credit is due: If you are sharing a certain truth or teaching, please share where you learned it. Some people become angry if you teach a lesson you have learned from them. I believe this is pride. If one of my young leaders teaches others with something they have learned from me, because it lives like a rhema (living) word in their hearts, then I pray they receive it like it is from the Lord Himself.

In my experience, believers benefit both from having someone to mentor them and having someone to mentor (if they are in a position to do that). So, you are being poured into by a mentor, and you are also pouring into someone else. Now, that's not going to be the case for you all the time, but it is definitely an encouragement and a blessing, and I would encourage you to seek that out.

APPLICATION

If you are not yet being mentored by someone and you seek that, bring that petition before the Lord. Ask Him to bring you a father or mother in the faith. Think of the people in your community who could fill that role and ask the Lord for clear direction. If it is the right fit, He will show you. Please don't fall into despair and declare, "There's just no one to mentor me!" Continually bring this request before God; He will find a way to train you.

If there is someone you feel would be a good fit, spend some time around them. It could be serving in the same capacity or asking them if they would be willing to meet you at a coffee shop or after a church service. Initiate the relationship. Many older believers just don't seek out younger people to train up because they (erroneously) assume their time and wisdom isn't needed. It may be on you to take this initiative and ask to meet.

Now, for future mentors: If you are approached by someone and you both pray about it, and it seems like a good fit, set the tone for consistency. You certainly don't have to meet every week, but set up a regular time when you will both be free to meet without distractions. Check up on your mentee between meetings. Understand that, in the beginning, they may require a bit more attention, but the goal is that they mature and grow beyond that. Stay patient, stay humble, stay consistent, and above all else, stay in the Word and in the presence of God.

AFTERWORD

Congratulations! You got to the end of the guide! It is now time to apply what you have learned. I want to encourage you to use what you have learned in your everyday life.

God wants you to make a difference in the lives of others on a regular basis. In my walk with God, I have met two categories of people: those who do and those who don't. There are some who are content to live a mundane Christian life. They are good people, nice to be around, but they have no ambition to be an agent of change to others and to the world around them.

Would you please accept the call to be one of "those who do"? Strive to grow every day in your walk with the Lord, and then take what you know and go out and shake the kingdom of darkness with what you've learned!

We are in the beginning stages of what some have called the great end-time harvest. That means that thousands of new believers are being swept into the Kingdom of God every day. These are people who know either nothing or very little about what you now know. We are going to need many laborers in the harvest field. Those new souls are going to need to be discipled! You can be part of that.

So I pray that you will let the last words of this guide send you forth to make a difference in God's Kingdom. Go and shake the world for Jesus!

NOTES

Chapter 1 The Voice of God

1. Wayne Grudem, *The Gift of Prophecy in the New Testament and Today* (Wheaton, IL: Crossway Books, 1988), 120.

Chapter 2 What Is the Goal of Prophecy?

1. Clifford Hill, *Prophecy Past and Present* (Ann Arbor, MI: Vine Books, 1989), 212.

Chapter 3 Preparing to Hear God's Voice

1. Quin Sherrer and Ruthanne Garlock, *A Woman's Guide to Breaking Bondages* (Ann Arbor, MI: Servant Publications, 1994), 116.
2. Noah Webster, *Webster's New Twentieth Century Dictionary* (New York: Simon and Schuster, 1979), 2100.
3. Dean Sherman, *Spiritual Warfare for Every Christian* (Seattle: Frontline Communications, 1990), 107.

Chapter 4 Is There a Protocol for Prophesying?

1. Webster, *Webster's New Twentieth Century Dictionary*, 1448.
2. Watchman Nee, *Spiritual Authority* (Richmond, VA: Christian Fellowship Publisher, 1972), preface.

3. C. Peter Wagner, *Your Spiritual Gifts Can Help Your Church Grow* (Ventura, CA: Regal Books, 1979; revised edition, 1994), 204, 206–207.

Chapter 5 Releasing the Prophetic Gift

1. Bill Hamon, *Prophets and Personal Prophecy* (Shippensburg, PA: Destiny Image Publishers, 1987), 120–123.

Chapter 6 Prophetic Callings and Prophetic Intercession

1. Norman Grubb, *Rees Howells, Intercessor* (Fort Washington, PA: Christian Literature Crusade, 1952), 40–41.

Chapter 7 Dreams and Visions

1. John Sandford and Paula Sandford, *The Elijah Task* (Tulsa, OK: Victory House, 1977), 187.

Chapter 8 I Need Help! Mentoring the Prophetic Gift

1. Dr. J. Robert Clinton, *The Making of a Leader* (Colorado Springs: NavPress, 1988), 130–131.

Cindy Jacobs is a prophet, speaker, teacher, and author with a heart for discipling nations in the areas of prayer and the prophetic. She and her husband, Mike, are the founders of Generals International, working to achieve social transformation through intercession and prophetic ministry. Cindy has written several bestselling books, including *Possessing the Gates of the Enemy*, *The Voice of God*, and *The Power of Persistent Prayer*. Cindy and Mike have a show called *Prophetic Dateline* that is streamed around the world through Instagram and Facebook. She travels and speaks internationally to groups of hundreds of thousands each year in churches and conference centers. Cindy and Mike have two grown children and six grandchildren and reside near Dallas, Texas.

cindyjacobsofficial

@cindymjacobs

More from Cindy Jacobs

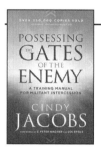

Practical, personal, biblical, and motivational, this bestselling book has sold over 250,000 copies and been a definitive go-to guide to intercessory prayer for years. Fully revised and updated, with an in-depth study guide, the fourth edition of this classic text offers new and vital insights and practical tips on spiritual warfare and praying effectively.

Possessing the Gates of the Enemy

In a world fraught with gender and relationship issues, the voices of women are needed more than ever. In this revised edition of a breakthrough book, bestselling author Cindy Jacobs speaks to the fears and insecurities women have about stepping up and speaking out, and she shows how to serve God faithfully, love others boldly, and change the world around you.

Women, Rise Up!